MARKETING
BUILT BY
L♥VE

MARKETING
BUILT BY
L♥VE

A Human-Centered Foundation to Delight Your Customers,
Increase Your Revenue, and Grow Your Business

DANIEL BUSSIUS

GREENLEAF
BOOK GROUP PRESS

Published by Greenleaf Book Group Press
Austin, Texas
www.gbgpress.com

Distributed by Greenleaf Book Group

For ordering information or special discounts for bulk purchases, please contact Greenleaf Book Group at PO Box 91869, Austin, TX 78709, 512.891.6100.

Design and composition by Greenleaf Book Group
Cover design by Greenleaf Book Group

Publisher's Cataloging-in-Publication data is available.

Print ISBN: 979-8-88645-092-7

eBook ISBN: 979-8-88645-093-4

To offset the number of trees consumed in the printing of our books, Greenleaf donates a portion of the proceeds from each printing to the Arbor Day Foundation. Greenleaf Book Group has replaced over 50,000 trees since 2007.

Printed in the United States of America on acid-free paper

23 24 25 26 27 28 29 30   10 9 8 7 6 5 4 3 2 1

First Edition

To my wife, Melissa, who has stood by my side throughout my crazy entrepreneurial journey

To my mother, who always believed in me and taught me that the difference between success and failure is if you give up or try again

To my son, who I hope will be inspired by this book to do anything he sets his mind to

To God, who has called me to do my best to add more love into this world

THE BEST THINGS IN LIFE
ARE BUILT BY LOVE

CONTENTS

PART III: Cultivating Long-Term Love

PART IV: Running on the RAMP

Foreword

THE CHALLENGES AND TRIUMPHS THAT SMALL businesses encounter in the ever-evolving world of marketing have been an integral part of my journey as the CEO of Keap. It's a landscape that is constantly shifting, with new tools and strategies emerging daily. For decades, we've recognized that customer relationship management (CRM) systems and automation can be powerful and transformative tools for businesses, but their true potential is realized only when they're coupled with a well-crafted marketing strategy. Unfortunately, many business owners become distracted by marketing hype, fads, and hacks, leading them to struggle with ineffective marketing efforts that leave them totally frustrated.

That is why, when I first learned about Daniel Bussius's approach to marketing, I was intrigued. *Marketing Built by Love* presents a fresh perspective that is grounded in neuroscience, psychology, and real-world experience. It addresses a fundamental truth that is often overlooked in the pursuit of the latest trends and tricks: at its core, marketing is about connecting with people. By acknowledging and embracing the humanity of our audience, we can create marketing campaigns that resonate on a deeper level and foster lasting relationships with our customers.

In this groundbreaking book, Daniel shares the four indispensable pillars of marketing success that are built on this foundational understanding of human nature. These pillars provide a road map for small business owners, marketers, and executives to create powerful and effective marketing strategies that truly connect with their audience. By aligning our marketing efforts with the science-based stages of human relationships, we can mimic the human experience in a way that cultivates customer loyalty and drives sustainable growth for our businesses.

Throughout my career, I have been privileged to witness the transformative power of marketing that is built on genuine connections and a deep understanding of human psychology. As one of Keap's top certified partners for many years, Daniel has consistently applied his methodology to transform our mutual customers' businesses. Simply put, when our customers combine automation with sound marketing principles, they experience wild success. In *Marketing Built by Love*, Daniel offers a framework that empowers businesses to tap into that power and achieve marketing success that is not only repeatable and consistent but also meaningful, authentic, and totally fulfilling.

This book is a game changer for business owners at all stages of business. It will challenge the way you think about marketing and provide you with the tools and strategies you need to create lasting impact for your business. I highly recommend reading and implementing what Daniel teaches within this book to anyone seeking a fresh, innovative approach to marketing that goes beyond superficial tactics and gets to the heart of what truly matters: our shared humanity.

CLATE MASK
CEO of Keap

Acknowledgments

FIRST AND FOREMOST, I THANK GOD for His grace in enabling me to overcome my mistakes with perseverance. I have rebounded with a focus centered on love rather than pain or anger.

I thank my family, beginning with my grandmother. Both my sense of humor and my desire to be an author come from her. I hope this makes her happy. I also thank my grandfather for showing me how to roll up my sleeves and get things done the best I can, even when I'm heading into the unknown and making it up as I go along. The principles Grandad taught this "California kid" have enabled me to do many of the things I've done, like rebuilding the engine of a '68 Volkswagen Bug or writing this book. My deepest appreciation also goes to my mother, who has shown me never-ending love and commitment, even when things seemed bleak. I know she has always believed in me, and I thank and love her for that.

I thank Brian and Carin Lazarus from Media Star Promotions in Baltimore, Maryland. They got me started in the world of experiential marketing. Without them, I'd likely never have discovered the incredible world of marketing. It was a discovery that led me to start my own agency on March 13, 1998.

I also thank the wonderful people at Keap, including but not limited to Jeremiah Sarkett, Matt Vosbourgh, Erin Case, Carmen Campbell, Clate Mask, and Scott Martineau. Their kindness, generosity, and belief in me were invaluable as my fledgling agency grew.

A big thanks also goes out to my incredible staff at Built by Love Agency, for serving our clients well and for helping build an amazing agency we can all be proud of.

Special thanks go to my editor, Stuart Horwitz, for helping me make my dream of turning the Marketing RAMP into a book a reality. Additionally, I am ever indebted to the wonderfully incredible team at Greenleaf Book Group: Sue, Brian, Rebecca, Anne, and Scott. This book would not have been possible without them.

A heartfelt thank-you goes out to my wife, who has stood by my side in the good times and the bad as I put in eighty-hour work weeks and traveled around the world, pushing to make this dream a reality. I know there were times when I was not present to help out, and I do not take her gracious understanding and faithfulness for granted. She inspires me, and she has blessed our family with an amazing son.

I want my son, Ocean, to know that he has the power to accomplish absolutely anything he dreams. There is nothing that can prevent him from making his wildest dreams come true as long as he believes in himself and never gives up. I encourage him to dream as big as he can. The right time to take bold action is always now. I love him, and I believe he can make the world a better place for humankind.

My final acknowledgment and appreciation go out to you, reader. I am grateful that you've invested your time with me, and I hope that the strategy and teachings contained within this book leave you inspired, help build your business stronger, and make the future look a little brighter.

I hope this book contributes to your greatest successes yet to come.

Marketing Is Broken (but We Can Fix It)

I know the ugly marketing truth and the secret that billion-dollar brands have known all along.

I HAVE TALKED TO COUNTLESS BUSINESS owners over the years who are frustrated that they're not getting the marketing results they're after. These are owners who lose money rather than make money when they invest in marketing. They might have hired a consultant, enlisted a marketing agency, or even invested in an entire in-house marketing team. Yet, they report to me time and time again that despite having put substantial resources into their efforts, the promised results never panned out. And, even more frustratingly, they are often unable to pinpoint where things went wrong.

That's because marketing is broken.

The problem isn't your business, what you're selling, or likely even your pricing. The problem is that traditional marketing no longer works in today's internet age of unlimited options, digital fatigue, and decreasing attention spans. Business owners and even most professional marketers have been duped by an industry filled with an endless array of empty promises founded on fundamentals that worked decades ago but have long since become useless.

The problem, from a technical standpoint, is that marketing is all about getting people into the sales process. That's it. How many qualified leads you are delivering to the business is typically the gauge for success or failure. It's rare for a marketing department to consider customer experience. That's not their job. Their concern is getting the highest conversion rates and sharpening the cost per conversion as much as possible. Basically, it becomes a matter of figuring out how they can get as many people as possible to buy a thing for maximum profit.

In the current ecosystem, it's almost as if marketing has been rigged for businesses to fail, especially the small business sector made up of people just like you and me who started a company to create a positive change in the world. The reality is that big corporations continue to exponentially grow, consuming their competitors, while small businesses flounder. The resources available to small business owners that they hope will better their chances at success—the conferences, the popular gurus, the trendy strategies bouncing around—encourage these businesses to invest in short-term marketing solutions that big brands don't bother with. Marketing professionals and agencies make money even when a small business's marketing efforts fail. This causes far too many businesses to get stuck in a frenzied cycle of chasing fruitless measures.

It's no wonder that so many small business owners have lost trust in marketing, feeling that anything and everything they've tried has failed to work. And they're probably right. If you're reading this book, you are likely an unfortunate participant in this marketing hell. So I must now ask you a question that I asked myself: *Are you tired of failing at marketing?*

I know I was.

I admit that I've had more marketing successes than failures over a decades-long career that included work with Fortune 500 brands, celebrities, *New York Times* best-selling authors, and small businesses from around the world. I've been part of some amazingly successful campaigns. The successes always feel great. I got it right, my clients made money, and everyone walked away happy.

I've also been part of some epic failures. Those rare times when a failure happened, the pain stung and never faded because I knew I'd not only let myself down but also let down the client who believed in me. That pain is what set me on a mission. I wanted to develop a marketing system that invariably generated sales and provided valuable insight for companies to make better business decisions.

TWO SIMPLE TRUTHS OF MARKETING

What I discovered in my decade of real-world research, having launched thousands of campaigns to millions of people across all continents of the world, is that the traditional marketing tactics businesses have been relying on for years are obsolete. Along the way, it became clear that most marketing efforts ignore two simple truths:

1. *Businesses need to have foundational marketing.* Billion-dollar brands already know the importance of having a comprehensive marketing plan that encompasses all the interactions between a business and its prospects and customers. They have an established marketing framework they don't mess with. That's what I think of as foundational marketing. From this core positioning, they are constantly creating content that engages their consumers and conveys variations of a consistent message tied to the business's purpose and value promise. The content addresses their consumers' internal objections, builds rapport, and inspires. Too many marketing professionals and agencies don't realize that the lack of a foundational marketing plan is why the clients or companies who hire them fall victim to a quest for results that never come.

2. *Marketing needs to be built around a love for the customer.* Customers want top-tier products and services. They want to be treated and acknowledged as human beings, not just another nameless sale. These are entirely reasonable expectations but ones that can prove surprisingly hard for businesses to deliver on. This is especially true if they don't act with intention and employ thoughtful strategies based on an understanding of customer needs and desires at every juncture of the buyer's journey.

Yet, despite these being relatively simple truths, most marketers haven't been taught these ideas. They don't realize that their chances of real success without having foundational marketing built around a love of customers are about as good as winning the lottery.

THE MARKETING RAMP: LESS CHAOS AND MORE PREDICTABILITY IN MARKETING

Have you noticed that all other business departments have proven systems they run on? They don't reinvent the wheel every month. Yet, marketing does just this. It's insanity! Can you imagine if every month your controller, accountant, or bookkeeper had an entirely new "strategy" to manage your money? You'd run for the hills. Yet, that's what's happening every day in every marketing agency meeting with their clients and inside marketing departments.

That's the challenge I set out to solve. I wanted to see if it was possible to have a marketing system that was *reliable, measurable,* and *repeatable*—terms not often associated with marketing. It took ten years of my life and cost more than a million dollars, but in the end, I built a system based on a foundational marketing approach and incorporating a love of customers that I call the *Marketing RAMP* (responsive, aligned master plan).

Think of a Marketing RAMP as the operating system you will use to shape the customer experiences you offer. These experiences will turn the prospects who can benefit most from your offerings into loyal customers. To build this operating system, you need to do a thorough analysis of factors such as the following:

- Characteristics (demographics, interests, etc.) of your best-fit customers

- What you are offering that will set you apart from competitors

- The language and stories that will create an emotional connection between them and you

- The steps your prospects go through from the moment they first encounter your brand to the decision to make a purchase

The system you create through your Marketing RAMP defines the system you will use to convert prospects into loyal customers. You'll learn specifics such as the following:

- The steps to follow, especially what gets programmed into your CRM (customer relationship management) system

- The decision points where different customer actions (or inactions) trigger different pathways through those steps

- The specific communications used to connect with your prospects at each step, including the language and tone needed to create ads, emails, and success stories that will resonate with the customers you want to attract

Because of this level of detail and specificity, the Marketing RAMP eliminates the chaos of traditional marketing funnels. It fills the gaps where you're losing money and customers, and it creates a centralized hub that produces predictable results. It will require determination and effort to get it going, but once a RAMP is in place, it is a powerful and lasting force.

THE HUMAN TOUCH

Unlike most traditional marketing efforts, the Marketing RAMP process spelled out in this book is imbued with an appreciation of how humans behave—specifically, how the human brain processes information, how humans develop relationships, and which experiences or touch points along the buyer's journey are key in guiding them to a successful outcome.

Your time and money invested in marketing will no longer be spent building funnels and generating new offers every month. Instead, your time in marketing will be focused on science, data, optimization, and engagement.

Once you get your foundation in place, you can trust that you have the marketing operating system you need to support leveling up. Rather than frantically spinning out marketing campaign after campaign intended to drum up leads, you can focus instead on cultivating genuine human connection and engagement that will lead to sustainable, organic growth. This will be better for you and better for your customers.

I know that the Marketing RAMP works because my business uses it. Using the Marketing RAMP system propelled my own award-winning digital marketing agency, Built by Love, to new heights of success. It has enabled us to help other business owners achieve the same in turn. Whether you're trying to break a million or a billion in revenue, this is the solution for you.

WHAT'S IN THIS BOOK

In this book, I walk you through how to build your own Marketing RAMP, so it can function as your marketing operating system today, tomorrow, and beyond. For that reason, I have also included exercises to craft your own marketing system, as well as blueprints to follow when you embark on building it. My intention for you is that you are empowered to do whatever your goals are with your business and that marketing is the last thing holding you back from achieving them. These pages contain my proven marketing operating system, which can be used to prosper enterprises of all sizes, anywhere in the world.

Part I, "Bringing Marketing into the Twenty-First Century," explores in more depth what is wrong with marketing today and introduces the four core principles—what I call pillars—of the responsive, aligned master plan (RAMP).

Part II, "Getting a Commitment from the Customer," discusses the first half (Stages 1 through 5) of the relationship journey that is embodied by the fourth pillar. The chapters talk about what you need to do to take a customer from a first date (where they get a first impression of you) to a commitment (where they make a first or repeat purchase).

Part III, "Cultivating Long-Term Love," covers the last half (Stages 6 through 10) of the relationship journey. The chapters explain what it takes to get a renewed or continuous commitment from your first-time buyers and how to convert those who have not yet purchased to take that step (or self-eliminate from your marketing system).

Part IV, "Running on the RAMP," provides an in-depth case study that shows how all the pieces of a Marketing RAMP come together and the steps you can take to start developing and implementing your own RAMP.

The formula laid out in these pages has universal applicability, no matter the size of your business, the industry you're in, your marketing budget, or where in the world you're based. It moves away from marketing centered around the product and instead taps into something timeless—almost primal—taking full consideration of what it is that makes us human. Rest assured, this isn't a quick fix or a trendy solution. Because it is an agile and living thing, the RAMP will work for you today, tomorrow, and decades from now.

BAD MARKETING VERSUS NO MARKETING

While it was the failure of marketing efforts that started me on this book-writing journey, I came to realize that some of the problems associated with *bad* marketing were also common to businesses that essentially have *no* marketing. True, bad marketing is in some ways worse because it involves misleading prospective customers about what your business is and what you provide. Ultimately, it leads to poor customer experiences. No marketing is marginally better because you're not communicating the wrong messages. But it, too, is ineffective because you aren't deliberately communicating anything to your prospects. In both situations, you are failing to connect with potential customers in ways that would lead to an increased revenue stream. The solution in both cases is to build a marketing system.

In many ways, the world of marketing has functioned like the Wild West, where anything goes and there's no one to enforce order. Well, it's time a new sheriff came to town, kicked out the hucksters, and paved a way that is safe for all businesses to follow. Hire a guide or don't; no longer will you be traveling in a wooden-wheeled wagon out West. You'll have a paved, efficient, and well-guided highway that gets you to the land of results no matter the size or speed that you travel to get there. This is the Marketing RAMP, and this will be your silver bullet to kill the marketing monster once and for all.

PART I

Bringing Marketing into the Twenty-First Century

SHORTLY AFTER MOVING TO SAN DIEGO, I decided to take up surfing. The first time I attempted to paddle out was a disaster. It didn't get much easier until I finally befriended some locals who taught me the ropes. They helped me understand the different and unique components of surfing I needed to understand before I experienced success in the water.

Before long, I knew to study the ocean before I jumped in. I knew to count the timing between each wave, to watch how they break, to take note of the lay of the land below the surface of the ocean, to be aware of the speed of the currents, and to see how far out the waves are beginning to curl. Only after gathering all this information was I able to paddle out successfully.

Like me, many beginners beeline straight for the water with their board only to get pummeled again and again, never getting past the wave break. Too many give up without ever experiencing the magic of surfing.

What they and you need to understand is what I learned many years ago. The work you do before you dip one toe into the ocean is what translates into success. It's important to identify and understand the moving parts, visualize the lay of the land, and see the method to the madness before you paddle out into the unknown. My job is to make sure that no matter what kind of wave comes your way, you'll be ready for it—and you'll enjoy the ride.

To get you started, this part of the book describes the underlying currents as well as the philosophy and principles that will shape your marketing efforts. Chapter 1 describes several fatal flaws in marketing systems today. Chapter 2 describes how establishing a Marketing RAMP can overcome the flaws. Chapters 3 through 7 describe the four parts of a Marketing RAMP and explore how each feeds into creating an effective marketing plan.

Starting in Chapter 3, most of the chapters are accompanied by exercises that will help you develop your own Marketing RAMP information.

CHAPTER 1

Five Fatal Flaws in Marketing Today

Traditional marketing has too many fatal flaws and
must be replaced with an integrated operating system.

LIKE ME, YOU THINK MARKETING IS BROKEN. You agree that, too often, marketing efforts do not deliver on their promise to attract new customers and build business. Understanding more about the ways in which it is broken will help establish the criteria for a better alternative. In this chapter, I talk about five fatal flaws in marketing today. In the next chapter, I talk about the solution I'm offering that avoids or fixes these flaws.

FLAW 1: MARKETING IS TOO TRANSACTIONAL

With the way marketing operates today, the process is very transactional. The ordinary executive in charge of your marketing is interested in numbers such as the following:

1. How much traffic are you generating each month to your offer pages? (These are the eyeballs of potential customers.)

2. What portion of this traffic becomes prospects? (Opting in for additional communication but no purchase yet.)

3. How many of the prospects who've opted in are purchasing, and what is the average time to buy? (Time to buy could be hours, days, or even months. The goal is to obtain new customers as fast as possible. Therefore, the cost of new customer acquisition in almost every case decreases.)

4. What is the cost of traffic versus the cost to convert those prospects into customers? (Cost of traffic is typically advertising costs but can be any activities designed to drive people to your business.)

5. Are you making a net profit, breaking even, or losing money on the acquisition of these new customers? (Understanding your true cost of acquisition plays into what your lifetime customer value is. You can usually afford to lose money acquiring customers if you have a high customer lifetime value with strong net profit margins.)

While data points like these are essential to make good business decisions, these questions are missing a critical factor. That omission is creating absolute chaos in every organization, and it is likely the key reason hundreds of millions, if not billions of dollars are wasted on fruitless marketing activities every single year. I guarantee that if you do marketing or run advertising campaigns, you have a black hole sucking money from your bottom line right now. Fixing this one thing should save you at least 20 percent in your annual marketing spend, if not more.

What's missing in every marketing campaign and subsequent data that marketers and advertisers are missing and blindly making wild guesses on is: *What do these leads and prospects actually want?* Marketers don't know, so they guess. And that guess comes in the form of "this person opted in for XYZ, so XYZ is their main interest." All communications and offers then force-feed XYZ to the new prospect, who has already cost you money to get to this point. Traditional marketing just keeps talking about and offering that one thing without ever asking them anything.

It's the twenty-first century, and marketing has to find a better balance between focusing on transactional numbers that feed into business decisions and developing a deeper knowledge of who your customers are and what they want, so you can grow revenues.

FLAW 2: IGNORING OUR REPTILIAN BRAINS

According to recent research, purchasing decisions are based more on emotion than on logic, no matter how structured we are in evaluating our options.[1] In fact, advertising campaigns that do the best have twice as much emotional content as rational content.[2]

Though we humans pride ourselves on using reason and logic in making decisions, the truth is much more complicated because our brains have three distinct components that evolved over the millennia. The oldest section is often called our reptilian brain. Then came structures associated with our mammalian brain. And finally, the most recent structures, labeled the logical human brain, are linked to our reasoning abilities (see Figure 1.1).[3]

All information must pass in order through each evolution of the brain, with the first one being the reptilian brain. This structure determines whether we need to pay attention to certain information. All it is concerned with are the basics of survival, which makes it lazy by design in order to preserve energy for matters of life and death.

---

1   Logan Chierotti, "Harvard Professor Says 95% of Purchasing Decisions Are Subconscious," *Inc.*, March 26, 2018, https://www.inc.com/logan-chierotti/harvard-professor-says-95-of -purchasing-decisions-are-subconscious.html.

2   USC Dornsife, "Thinking vs Feeling: The Psychology of Advertising," accessed February 10, 2023, https://appliedpsychologydegree.usc.edu/blog/thinking-vs-feeling-the -psychology-of-advertising/.

3   Paul D. MacLean, *The Triune Brain in Evolution* (New York: Springer, 1990).

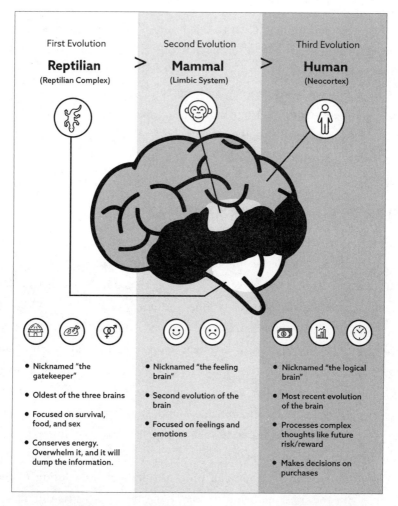

Figure 1.1. Three evolutions of the human brain.

I call the reptilian brain the gatekeeper. And too often, marketing and sales information doesn't get past that gate. We approach a prospect with complex information at the start or give too much too quickly and overwhelm them. Their reptilian brains will likely decide that too much energy is required to process it, and your message will evaporate into the air. In other words, it doesn't matter how beautifully crafted or logical your messages are. You need to connect emotionally with a customer or prospect.

The existence of the reptilian brain helps bring context to just how wrong a traditional marketing approach gets it, entirely ignoring how humans engage and process information. Suppose I send you correspondence that says, "Hey. How's it going? I'm Daniel, and I can help you with marketing. You and I should work together. Commit here because time is running out!" Your reptilian brain will immediately sound the alarm and filter the risk away.

PREVIEW: THE RIGHT INFORMATION IN THE RIGHT SEQUENCE

As I talk about later in the book, the existence of these different parts of the brain is also a factor in how humans move from noncommitted to committed relationships. For our purposes as marketers, not only do we need to say the right thing to get a prospective ideal customer to pay attention, but we also must do the right things in the right order to move them from a stranger to someone who is interested in us and eventually falls in love with us. This is science, and if we fail to follow those processes that humans do when forming bonds, we'll never form a bond with those ideal customers we want to have committed relationships with. You can find more details on this relationship journey in Chapter 7 and throughout Parts II and III.

To get through the gatekeeper in people's brains, we must earn customers' trust and address their fears. We need to be able to connect with our customers and prospects in ways that engage the gatekeeper in their brains. Putting your customers at ease in this way matters. People make decisions based on emotion. We're talking about all decisions here, not just buying decisions. We probably all know a steady, rational person who insists they make their choices based entirely on logic. I don't dispute that reasoning certainly plays a part. But I maintain that everything humans do is based primarily on emotion that may or may not be backed up by logic.

Put simply, the fix to this flaw is that before diving into the details of what's on offer, marketers need to make sure that the reptilian brain has concluded that our message is worth investing in.

FLAW 3: FUNNELS ARE DEAD

The marketing funnel is dead. The sales funnel is dead, too. Well, at least the traditional funnels you're using now are long-outdated strategies. A simple example illustrates why.

Consider what goes through your mind when you make plans to eat out. You might think, "We should eat at that Mexican restaurant we like. But no, wait. I really like that quaint French restaurant across town. Then again, since the weather is so nice, let's just go to that bistro that has the great outdoor patio. . . ." For most of us, our thoughts dart all over the place before we're able to commit to where we'll dine. We change our minds as we learn more. Perhaps your dinner companion says they heard the French restaurant has doubled its prices. Or maybe the weather turns colder and windy. So, after initially choosing the bistro, you circle back to the Mexican restaurant as your dining choice.

Imagine, then, what this process looks like when the decision has to do with something much more expensive, or with otherwise larger stakes. How people perceive their choices and ultimately reach a decision is seldom a simple process.

Yet, traditional funnels are robotic. They don't consider how humans behave and interact. A funnel will talk at you, shouting the same message on loop with unrelentless, automated energy. Not only does it not care about your response, but it also doesn't even register that you could have a response. All it cares about is the sale. Funnels are a hammer that perceives everyone they interact with as a nail. There is no back and forth, no two-way communication, and no exploration of what the customer is really after. They are linear and focused on transactions. This does not comfortably coexist with humans, who are complex and motivated by myriad thoughts and feelings.

People tend to bounce around in unpredictable patterns before they make commitments. Traditional funnels don't allow for this, and that quickly becomes irritating and unproductive for both the business and the consumer. The funnel sets forth a linear path that rests on the incorrect assumption that a prospect's purchase behavior will never deviate from seeing your product as the only option and as the single highest priority in their life. You and I both know that makes absolutely no sense.

Because of their unyielding and unrealistic nature, funnels create opportunity gaps, and opportunity gaps are where you hemorrhage cash and drive prospects away. Even the customers who somehow make it to the end of the funnel reach the end of the line and drop off a cliff, unlikely to ever return. That is obviously not what we want or what our businesses need.

DO YOU HAVE A HEALTHY FLOW OF LEADS?

My guidance around the customer journey strategies assumes that your business has an ongoing flow of prospects waiting to hear from you. The healthy flow of leads into your business is the only fuel that can power your sales machine. That sales machine is what provides sustenance to your business's survival. Without sales, your business will starve. Without marketing, you won't have sales. It's an intricately intertwined balance of your business life, and every part is equally important. One must have the other. Eliminate one, and the other begins to die. In the end, your business succumbs to entropy.

If your business's inability to generate a large number of quality leads is one of your top concerns, you need to fix that problem. Consider working with a professional agency if your company does not have the internal

continued

expertise to make it happen. Engaging with a team of seasoned experts in their respective crafts—copywriting, advertising, web design, and marketing systems—provides invaluable insight into where you are with your current lead-generation efforts and what might change to produce better results.

FLAW 4: A DECADE (OR MORE) BEHIND TECHNOLOGY

The traditional marketing and sales funnel models just discussed were designed when the internet was early in its development—not for the widely diverse digital world we have now filled with unlimited information, resources, and options.

Then, the online behavior of consumers looked entirely different than it does today. If someone ended up on a website and opted in to something, it was likely because they had specifically searched it out, and it held a high priority for them. It was an effective strategy for the business to then hammer the consumer with emails saying, "Buy this thing! And this thing! And this thing!"

However, the world and its technologies have become far more complex since the concept of the funnel was originally introduced. There are overwhelming options now. But even beyond being inundated with choice, there have been other wild developments. For example, algorithms are so advanced that they can pick up when the person you live with checked out sneakers online and then target you with ads for shoes, assuming you're going shopping together because of your phones' GPS data showing your proximity. The point is we're not playing in the same arena as ten years ago. We're hardly even playing the same sport. Why, then, would we think that the digital marketing approach created in the internet's infancy would still be relevant today?

Using the marketing funnel as your guiding modus operandi not only is outdated and out of touch but also can and will do active harm. To put the marketing funnel's methodology into a real-world scenario: Imagine a consumer is walking down the street, and I ask, "Can you give me some money?" When no answer comes, I try again. "Sir, can you give me some money?" Silence. "Please, can you give me some money?" If they keep walking and continue to ignore me, it's obvious my tactic isn't working. And why should they stop and give me their time, attention, or money when I haven't proven I can offer them something of value?

If we want to be effective, we need to change this dynamic. Although it sounds ironic, we need to use technology better so we can humanize our interactions with our customers.

FLAW 5: UNSTRUCTURED CHAOS

As I mention in the introduction, the marketing process in any business seems to be the most unorganized and chaotic. Allow me to elaborate.

When you look at other departments within a successful business, you'll see that each has a well-defined operating system dictating exactly how each process needs to happen. The operating system also identifies key performance indicators (KPIs) as well as budgets, labor, and resource allocations.

Think of the finance department. There is an operating system in place for all expenses and payments. Your business lunch last week with a prospective customer? That is categorized under meals and entertainment. Your new mouse pad and keyboard you purchased? Office supplies. Your paycheck? Wages and compensation.

It makes sense that every part of a healthy business has an operating system, yet there's one major gaping hole sucking the wind out of all the other departments. This black hole is your marketing department that has no operating system. Every month, it's a new tactic, tool, or channel being implemented with no foundational system guiding the choices. A marketing department too often feels like a hamster wheel where insanity not only lives but thrives.

The goal must be to tame this beast and install an operating system that empowers the creatives within the department to focus on what they should be doing—generating content that engages your customers and optimizes the operating system to extract better results, conversions, customers, and profits.

The benefit of having an operating system is that it produces predictable results for those running the system and those on the other end experiencing the system. You better believe that a production line at a manufacturing plant has an operating system that all must follow to ensure production output meets or exceeds quality, profitability, and forecasted standards. Even sales departments have an operating system on how they sell, what they say, what can be offered, who has authorization to discount, and types of accounts that specific reps can engage with. Shouldn't marketing do the same?

THE FIX TO THESE FLAWS

The discussion of these flaws should make it clear what attributes I looked for when developing a new marketing approach:

- Adding a human element that will form a balance to the transactional side of marketing

- Taking the human brain into consideration when shaping the marketing process and communications with customers

- Replacing a mindless funnel with a more deliberate process for shepherding customers through the buying process

- Improving the use of technology to make the process more individualized but still automatic

- Developing a repeatable process that would replace chaos with order and predictability

In the next chapter, I give an overview of how the Marketing RAMP system achieves these goals.

TOP TAKEAWAYS

1. Traditional marketing approaches suffer from fatal flaws that limit their effectiveness, and they are the cause of widespread disappointment with marketing efforts as well as poor customer experiences.

2. It is time to leave the traditional (read: outdated) marketing funnel model in the past where it belongs.

3. Marketing too often ignores how the human brain operates and how that influences human behavior.

4. Marketing need not be a mysterious black hole with unreliable results. There is a strategy out there that leads to consistent, reliable results that will leave both you and your customers feeling good.

5. All businesses need a marketing operating system—otherwise, you will continue to fail while you are spending even more money.

CHAPTER 2

From New Leads to Raving Fans: The Promise of a Marketing RAMP

Replacing traditional marketing with
human-centered experiences is the key.

I'VE TALKED ABOUT THE FLAWS OF marketing in its current state—static and unrelenting funnels, outdated use of technology, messages that fail to get past the gatekeeper, and chaotic and unstructured operations. The fix to these flaws is the Marketing RAMP, a *responsive, aligned master plan* on which all marketing efforts rest. It defines a strategic sequence of communications, actions, and experiences with one overarching aim: transforming your new leads into raving fans.

The Marketing RAMP systematizes marketing, sales, and customer experiences. It taps into the core human process of decision-making by constantly considering how our customers feel and where they are at in their relationship stage with our brand. Delivering quality products and services to our clients is only half of our obligation as a business.

We will never maximize our potential as organizations or as individuals if we fail to recognize that the customer journey (how what we do makes our customers feel every step of the way) is the other half. We will never build the trust or forge the loyalty that we're looking for with our customers.

The rest of this book describes the details of what a Marketing RAMP is and how it can deliver on the "raving fans" promise. This chapter is a preview of the big picture of a Marketing RAMP and why it is superior to traditional marketing approaches.

THE RAMP FRAMEWORK

The components of the Marketing RAMP are built around three considerations of how people actually behave:

1. How human brains function and assign worth

2. How humans form organic relationships

3. How these things work together to transform your brand from its simple existence as just another commodity into an appreciated asset

By addressing these elements of neurology, the RAMP will help convert what prospects may see as a commodity—something that meets a simple need and is selected based on price and overall ease of accessibility—into an asset that offers true and ongoing value. Commodities get the job done, whereas assets elicit emotional connection and a sense of importance. People are willing to invest resources and energy into assets, and that's the goal. It is impossible to state the value of a customer who has formed a deep and meaningful relationship with your brand.

The RAMP is broken into four segments or primary pillars (see Figure 2.1). Within each pillar is a subset of rules and frameworks designed to failproof your marketing success.

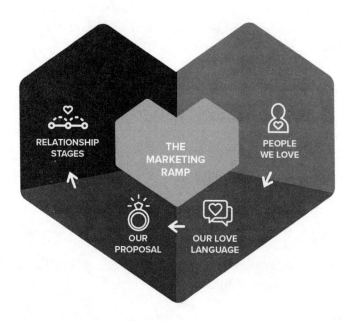

Figure 2.1. The four pillars of the Marketing RAMP.

Pillar 1: People We Love

The RAMP will get you clarity on the prospects your business needs to focus on. We call these people the *people we love*.

This first pillar is focused on identifying the customers we want to be serving. These are the people we're sure would love what we're providing if only we were able to reach them and make them our customers. In other words, these are the people who will help our business flourish. There are several marketing terms out there to describe this group of people: target demographic, avatars, and buyer personas. In this book, I call this group the ideal customers. While the general concept is widely present in available marketing material, the way the RAMP profiles ideal customers focuses on people or businesses who have struggles that we can alleviate better than anyone else. If you are clear about the people you love and their interests and pains, then you will be able to connect with them more easily.

Pillar 2: Our Love Language

Next, the RAMP will guide you through the process of communicating with the people you love so you can connect with them using the right words and the right language. We call this *our love language.*

The second pillar within the Marketing RAMP is the way in which our brand communicates with our ideal customers. This goes deeper than simply cultivating a brand voice. It's about creating an entire language, one that fosters true connection and eliminates missed connections. It's about making your customers feel seen, known, and supported. Later, we discuss why every part of how you communicate—the structure, the tonality, the formality—affects whether you're able to connect with your ideal customer or not. We also explore how to make sure you are indeed speaking the same language as your audience.

Pillar 3: Our Proposal (Our Brand Pitch)

Once we know the people we love and our love language, the RAMP's framework will develop your brand pitch to help you stand out from your competition by stating why the customer should buy from you. This is called *our proposal.*

The third pillar in the Marketing RAMP is how we package our brand for our ideal customers. Crafting an effective brand pitch requires first understanding and articulating what makes our brand special, what our superpowers are, and what we should be talking about. Then, the gaze turns outward. What are our competitors' strengths? How do they differ from ours? How can that be put in a positive light? The refined RAMP formula will help you figure this out. It provides the exact right words in the most powerful combination to be used across your sales and marketing assets, everywhere from your website to formal presentations to casual conversations.

Pillar 4: Relationship Stages (the Customer Journey)

The last part of the RAMP harnesses the scientific stages of how humans develop relationships[4] and overlays that with the buyer's journey and how marketing should interact with buyers along that journey. These stages then become the core of the Marketing RAMP, where the information from the previous three pillars is used to develop your very own marketing operating system.

I have defined the ten master stages that have been built to mirror the scientific phases of human relationships, letting us tap into something inherent and organic present in all human beings rather than ineffectively force-feeding them through the funnel (see Figure 2.2).

Figure 2.2. The ten dynamic customer journey stages of the Marketing RAMP.

---

4 Mark L. Knapp and Anita L. Vangelisti, *Interpersonal Communication and Human Relationships* (Boston: Allyn and Bacon, 2009).

A TIMELESS SOLUTION

The Marketing RAMP is nothing like traditional marketing today, but it's everything that it should be. It treats humans like humans, following the laws that shaped the evolution of our species. People are complex and erratic, and the RAMP allows for that. Because of this, many of the concepts and stages within it overlap. Some occur simultaneously, others are contingent on a specific combination of earlier steps having taken place, and still others loop back to earlier stages according to customer response. The RAMP keeps track of each movement, making sure the customer is where they need to be and hearing what they need to hear.

The RAMP will specify exactly which customers you are going to pursue, why you will pursue them, and the best ways to do so. It will allow you to reshape your CRM to be more effective and in better alignment with customer buying behavior and digital experiences. Every single piece of the process is built to engage with humans wherever they're at in their own life journey and to create a valuable and unique experience tailored to their needs.

The Marketing RAMP is a formulaic approach you can rely on as your core truth and guiding light, but one that can also be customized to exactly suit your business and further its success. By creating and implementing a Marketing RAMP, your efforts will increase in stability and predictability while remaining flexible and responsive.

Every part of the RAMP has been designed with a purpose. It will take time to implement, and there will be a certain amount of front-loaded effort and investment to get it up and running (just like any asset you'd buy for your business). But once you've built your marketing foundation, you will feel the positive effects immediately and indefinitely. New leads will start to surface more frequently and from a wider variety of sources. The positive reviews and customer testimonials will come flowing in. You will begin to generate momentum.

Better yet, the RAMP is designed to be timeless. Too many of the marketing strategies that I come across feel like the next fad diet. There's always a sense of urgency even in how they're communicated: "You've got to try this!" or "You've never seen anything like this before!" or "The only thing that actually works!" I sometimes feel embarrassed to be in the marketing world when I come across one of these claims so layered in marketing jargon and shouted promises you can hardly understand them. I decided to channel that into building something that can benefit all businesses and stand the test of time. The RAMP will work for any brand anywhere in the world, regardless of what they're selling, who they're selling to, what vertical they're in, or if they're making ten thousand a year or ten billion a year in revenue.

The Marketing RAMP is your engine and your operating system. Leads will fuel your engine, and from that fuel, the RAMP will create a forward motion for your business, churning out new customers, raving fans, and sales. Knowing the fundamentals of how this engine works empowers you to diagnose, repair, and build any marketing engine within any business.

This universality and adaptability of the RAMP means that its strategy holds sound even when up against the unexpected. In 2019, I started work with a company that had been selling physical education curriculum to school systems for the last twenty years but had never been able to surpass half a million dollars in gross revenue. The owner decided that she was ready to smash through that figure and reach a new level of success, so she reached out to my agency, Built by Love. We advised her that she needed a complete overhaul—everything from her website to her sales collateral to her marketing to the story she was telling her prospective clients and customers. What she needed was the Marketing RAMP.

The owner was hesitant at first. Because she was working with public school systems and ritzy private schools, the sales process was complex and required convincing multiple people to sign off and say yes. How could our Marketing RAMP truly serve her business and her customers?

We revamped her entire process, and customers provided immediate feedback that they loved the experience, the messaging, and the simplified way the company now laid out the service it provided and its benefits. Things were off to an amazing start, and the owner and her team couldn't have been happier that they decided to adopt the RAMP.

Then, the pandemic hit. As the virus swept through the country, everything—schools included—was shut down for months. The owner was understandably worried. How could she sell physical education programs to schools if schools were closed and students had to stay at home?

Because the Marketing RAMP was already built and in place, it made it incredibly easy for her when she decided to pivot to selling online courses. The RAMP had been in play for several months, doing the work of nurturing new and existing leads, moving them through the right stages toward a sale, and delivering delight in every touch point along the way. In a year that saw many of her competitors file for bankruptcy, the owner achieved the original goal that brought her to us. For the first time in her twenty years in business, amid a pandemic that should have directly harmed her bottom line, that business owner broke through the barrier and made a million dollars.

That's what I want for you. I want you to walk away from this book equipped with a proven plan that works, feeling clarity around how to implement it and hope regarding what it means for your business down the line. I want you to walk into the future boldly, feeling like you have the best strategy in place no matter what is thrown at you. I have done my best to demystify marketing and break an effective strategy into small, manageable pieces in the following chapters. If you put in the time and dedication, marketing success will be something you can accomplish on your own.

FROM COMMODITY TO VALUED ASSET

The goal of implementing a Marketing RAMP is to have customers view your offerings as valued assets rather than commodities. But the RAMP itself can become an asset for your business, just like a real piece of machinery or a vehicle or intellectual capital. Like any business asset, it may cost some time, effort, and money to get it running, but it will perpetually produce profits once in place. It is a wise investment and one that every business should make for its marketing department.

Your business can be empowered by adopting this foundational master plan that eliminates dead-end funnels and gaps in buyers' journeys. This allows your teams to direct their focus toward reaching wider audiences and serving them well.

You should now have an understanding of the RAMP's four core pillars, and that the fourth pillar includes ten stages tied to the buyer's journey. It's time for us to get into the good stuff. The next chapter invites you into the first pillar, where you master how to implement it within your business for marketing clarity and success. Let's dive in.

 TOP TAKEAWAYS

1. The RAMP is made up of four core pillars:

   a. The people we love = our ideal customers—these people are most likely to struggle with challenges or pain that we are ideally suited to resolve

   b. Our love language = a system of communication—how we will speak to our ideal customers

   c. Our proposal = our brand pitch—how to best communicate our offers and explain why they should commit to us

   d. Relationship stages = the stages of the buyer's journey—a pillar with ten stages designed to mimic how humans form relationships

2. Once your RAMP is in place, it handles all the hard organizational work that underpins effective marketing so that you don't have to worry.

3. A Marketing RAMP will be useful only if it is timeless, providing a framework that will last for years while also being flexible enough to adapt to the changing needs of a business.

4. Your Marketing RAMP should be considered an asset to your business.

CHAPTER 3

RAMP Pillar 1: The People We Love (Our Ideal Customers)

Identifying whom the business must love, our ideal customers, and how we can win their love is the first pillar of every successful marketing campaign.

IMAGINE YOU OWN AN ICE CREAM SHOP. Everybody loves ice cream, right? So, you might argue, "Everybody is my customer." While yes, in theory, anybody and everybody could buy ice cream, does that knowledge help you keep your business afloat? Nope. One goal of your marketing efforts is to identify the people who, if they were to show up every day, would help guarantee your business thrives. That is not "everybody." It is the happy customers, the loyal customers, the kind that your staff love because they never cause problems, and the kind that write you glowing reviews.

These are the *people we love*, also known as *ideal customers*. Identifying these people is the first pillar of the Marketing RAMP (see Figure 3.1). These ideal customers are at the heart of everything, and effective marketing hinges on developing a deep understanding of your customer base.

Figure 3.1. The first pillar of the Marketing RAMP.

So who are these people you should love? Beginning in this chapter and continuing in subsequent chapters, I explain everything you need to know to identify, understand, and communicate with the people your business will best thrive by serving.

YOUR BUSINESS'S TRIBE

When you've found yourself at a concert, sporting event, or comedy club in the past, have you noticed how being in a crowd changes the experience? Does live music move you more than listening to the same artist at home by yourself? Is the big game more intense when you're at the stadium than watching from your couch? Do you laugh out loud at a live comedy performance but only quietly chuckle when watching the same comedian on TV?

The reason for this is the power of being surrounded by people who are similar to you and who reflect and multiply the intensity of your positive emotions back at you. When a group—or *tribe*—of people all share the same passion, that makes for a better experience for everyone involved. These people are the musician's, sports team's, or comedian's ideal customers, and it is this group that makes their product so much more enjoyable to consume. That is why it's important for every business to find its ideal customers and learn how to speak directly to them.

The construct is simple: we are defining a prototype of the person your company does business with most frequently. This could be modeled after current customers or be the profile of the person the company wants to become their new ideal customer.

You've probably heard the term "ideal customer" and may have even used the concept. But too many businesses rush through this work. Marketers seem to most often either give the concept of ideal customers the bare minimum or else invest their energy in the wrong place. They sit around a boardroom and put an imaginary face and personality to that person: "This is Sally, the homeowner. Age thirty-five and with two kids under the age of ten." I don't see much value in that. It's not going to make it into copy.

The most common templates, often seen in college textbooks and employed by nearly every marketer to identify their ideal customer, are insufficient and fail to collect all the pieces of the profile necessary for success. While getting in the weeds is rarely productive in life or business, not asking the right questions—or enough questions—means building an incomplete profile of an ideal customer. This is hardly better than no profile and will lead to you having the wrong conversations with your prospects, resulting in fewer customers, fewer sales, and fewer opportunities.

Superficiality is a mistake. If you incorrectly or incompletely define your ideal customer, it doesn't matter how creative and compelling your marketing is. You might think you're reaching everybody when in fact you're really reaching nobody. We want to go deep but keep it simple: this is our ideal customer, and this is their problem.

Conversely, if you carefully study the salient characteristics of the people doing business with you or the people you are targeting as potential clients, you gain a meaningful understanding of who they are and can communicate with them far more effectively.

IDENTIFYING WHO YOUR IDEAL CUSTOMERS ARE

If you don't know who your ideal customers are, you need to sit down and figure that out. Consider the Pareto principle of 80/20, where 20 percent of the population—or maybe even less—are giving you 80 percent or more of your revenue. Whatever you're doing right now is really resonating with them, and it benefits you to drill down on who they are and how and why they interact with your company.

EVEN START-UPS HAVE IDEAL CUSTOMERS

For start-ups that don't yet have a customer base, it's crucial that they vet their business idea and go to market with an ideal customer in mind. Much like the ice cream shop owner, a start-up with a new product might be tempted to say, "I think everyone will like this." Hopefully, one day in the future, that'll be true. But if you're starting from nothing, you better have a specific ideal customer in mind. If you're not sure who to serve, bring it back to what you love. If you're passionate and you're an expert in that area, then you're going to want to serve those people who will benefit most from your passion and expertise.

Large companies might use online forms to home in on their ideal customer. They might enlist a third-party firm that does data analysis across multiple sources to provide enriched profiles. Or they might conduct focus groups or run pilot programs in certain markets to gather feedback. However, defining ideal customers need not be an elaborate or expensive effort. It's okay if you don't have the financial firepower and the time it takes to pull off this level of detail.

In fact, a lot of the methods employed by companies at this scale are flawed. Take focus groups, for example. There is a unique dynamic at play when humans gather, each bringing a different personality type. Typically, there are going to be one or two dominant participants, and they're going to take on a leadership role in the focus group. They become the spokesperson and, inevitably, they sway the group. There could be someone in the focus group who doesn't really like strawberry ice cream, but the de facto leader declares, "Strawberry is by far the best choice." Suddenly, that other person finds themselves saying, "Yeah, I guess strawberry is the best. That's fine." There's incredible room for error in a focus group environment. Opinions are very easily tainted.

There are ways to combat that if you're a corporation with unlimited funds. But many times, businesses fail because they invest too much in focus groups rather than taking the Pareto principle to heart and mining their existing data for the guiding information they need. Who are the people buying from you most frequently? Who are the people spending the most money with you? Who is continually repeat buying? If you spend enough time with this data, you're going to see a trend. There's no reason to jump straight into investing tens of thousands of dollars on research when you haven't even explored the completely free information that's already in your possession.

The goal, simply put, is to get a holistic view of your customers. There are four aspects of an ideal customer profile that you should explore (see Figure 3.2). Yes, it's important to gather basic *demographics*—age, gender, ethnicity, income—but there are other layers that can be mined for a deeper understanding, such as their *interests*, their *pain points* (where they've struggled in areas related to your offering), and their *relationship* with your business.

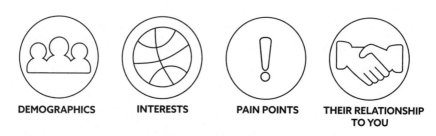

Figure 3.2. Four key parts of the ideal customer.

As you begin to flesh out information in each of these areas, you want to stay in the sweet spot with parameters that are neither too narrow nor too wide-reaching. If a message is too targeted, you miss out on potential clients. If it gets too broad, you dilute your message, and it loses its impact. By painting a picture of your ideal customers, you can see where they are coming from, which will help you understand what their problems are and how you can help solve them.

Exercise 1, at the end of this chapter, lists the specific questions you should answer in each of these four areas. To help you understand the fuller context, let me explore each of these areas in more depth.

BASIC DEMOGRAPHICS

Let's start thinking through who your ideal customer is by asking questions such as the following:

- What is their age range?
- Where do they live?
- What do they do for a living?

Consider age, for example. The standard ideal customer age range should be about ten years. If you carry out this exercise and decide that your ideal customer age span is eighteen to twenty-one or, conversely, eighteen to sixty-nine, I'd encourage you to reconsider.

Suppose I ask an ice cream shop owner who their ideal customer is. They could confidently answer that kids are their ideal customers because kids eat the most product. That would be wrong. Kids don't have money. It's not a kid who walks in with his whole baseball team to buy all fifteen a scoop. Instead, kids are indirect recipients of the treat. They might appeal to an adult to bring them in, sure, but ultimately it is their parent or guardian's decision to stop at the store and buy ice cream. Suddenly, it becomes clear that parents aged thirty-five to forty-five (remember, you want about a ten-year age span) are your ideal customers. They often come in with one or more kids, and they tend to spend a lot of money. Targeting this group will help you create a reliable, loyal fan base of customers.

TARGETING, NOT EXCLUSION

There will be customers on the fringes who don't fall under our ideal customer profile, and we certainly aren't trying to exclude them. The ice cream shop will still warmly welcome a sixty-five-year-old grandad who comes in on his own on his afternoon walk to buy a cone. Identifying your ideal customer has nothing to do with excluding certain people from your goods or services. No one is being barred from entry. Rather, it's about figuring out which people are most likely to come in, be satisfied, and come back many times over.

So will that sixty-five-year-old grandad be who you keep in your mind as you develop your marketing plan? Is he whom you think of as you name the ice cream flavors? No. You're going to generate material that is geared around appealing to parents and maybe their kids indirectly. Naming a flavor the Sugarblaster may excite a kid, but the parent is going to say, "No way. Not in a million years." So you name it Berry Blast instead, and everybody is happy.

GETTING TO KNOW YOUR IDEAL CUSTOMERS ON A DEEPER LEVEL

Even if you have a detailed demographic description of your ideal customer, it can sometimes be hard to ascertain what's driving a client base. You need to understand their belief systems, what motivates them, and what interests them.

For example, let's say we've identified that the ideal customer for our business is a woman aged thirty to forty. As we collect more data, we see that our ideal customer is also married, has two children under the age of ten, and tends to have at least one pet. The ideal customer is college educated, owns her home, and lives in or around Annapolis, Maryland.

We now know the makeup of our ideal customer. That is powerful, but there needs to be more. We want to explore what the ideal customer wants, how they perceive themselves, what keeps them from attaining what they want, and how we can offer a solution. That's where the other three parts of the profile for an ideal customer—interests, pain points, and relationship to you—come in. Exploring these areas will help you zero in on what it is these customers want and why.

Interests

Remember that one of the goals of marketing, as defined by the RAMP, is to connect with people at an emotional level. We must hit the triggers in their reptilian brain, so they will be more open to hearing reasons and facts associated with why they should buy from you. One way to make such connections is to study what interests your ideal customers. You want to answer questions such as the following:

- What do they want?
- How do they perceive themselves?
- What is their idea of success?
- What do they value?

- What prevents them from achieving what they want?
- Where do they live online? (News, education, entertainment, etc.)
- Who or what influences their decisions?

Pain Points

No matter your business's size, background, or organizational structure, you must figure out what the biggest problem is that your ideal customer has and how you can help solve it. This goes hand in hand with identifying your ideal customer. We dive more deeply into this topic later in the RAMP process, but here at the beginning, it is helpful to study your ideal customer's past actions and consider questions such as the following:

- Have they tried to fix this problem before and failed?
- Did they have bad experiences with a competitor's solution?
- How did these past unsuccessful endeavors make them feel?
- What objections might they have to making a purchase based on their past experiences?

This history of their behavior, the failure they may have faced, and their accumulated emotions all work to shape their internal talk track. This, in turn, shapes their internal objections, which could make them resistant to change and closed off from listening to your messages. In other words, just because your product or service can help someone and they may even trust you, they still may not buy from you until their internal objections have been met with counterarguments. Those objections likely arise from prior failures of the previous solutions they tried.

By way of a preview, think about internal objections you will need to overcome as you work to build a relationship with a prospective buyer, which is the subject of Pillar 4 (see also Part II). For now, it's important to know that the internal talk track is the inner voice all people have that narrates their lives and informs their actions and decisions.

Evolutionarily, this voice is there to help us survive by steering us clear of risk and the possibility of pain. But while the intention of the inner voice is to protect us, it is, by design, focused on the negative rather than the positive. Fear and pain keep us cautious and alert, which keeps us alive. Often, this negative inner voice becomes more foe than friend as it holds us back from taking actions that may improve our lives. Being able to describe pain points and how your company solves them is a theme woven throughout all aspects of the Marketing RAMP.

Relationship to You

Once you establish a clear idea of who your ideal customer is, you can discover more things about them specifically related to what will influence their relationship with your business. This includes questions such as the following:

- What kinds of solutions are they looking for?
- How will purchasing your product/service define them?
- What business have they done with you in the past, if any?
- Have they had interactions with your company but *not* made a purchase?

One strategy for answering these questions is to categorize your existing content. Look at what kind of content you have been putting out through your website, your social media, your ads, or your digital communications. Now, assemble a list of the major topics you address. If you can then track what your customers are clicking on, you can start to figure out what your ideal customers are most interested in. That helps you drill down on who's attracted to your content, what kind of help they likely need, and what to emphasize more strongly in your future messaging.

If you're a relatively small enterprise, or if you have a brick-and-mortar storefront, there is the additional option of interacting with and observing clients in person. An easy exercise to start with is pulling security camera footage to watch through on fast-forward. Over time, you will see a trend of what type of people most commonly frequent your store and what they do while there (what draws attention, purchases they make, etc.). Gathering information straight from customers is another easy way to home in on their motivations.

Going back to the ice cream shop example, you might ask a customer, "What brought you in today?" A dad could answer, "My kid scored a goal at his soccer game today. We're celebrating!" Or a mom might reply, "My daughter got a perfect score on her test." Over time, you will start to see the ritual at play. When kids perform well, their parents want to celebrate and reward them, and that just so happens to often be with ice cream.

Knowing that, you can run a special marketing campaign with the implicit message of "Your child's achievements should be celebrated." You can encourage parents that any time their child does something great—gets an A on a report card, finishes a book, handles a tough thing well—they can mark that moment with an ice cream treat to make it even more special. Maybe you even have a deal where if a kid scores a goal, they get a free ice cream. Humans are ritualistic beings, so knowing what rituals your ideal customers already do or would enjoy doing plays into your business's favor and can be injected within your Marketing RAMP.

BE CREATIVE IN REACHING OUT

Even if you're a digital company, you're not barred from doing on-the-ground research. If you're a small business, you can reach out to your big, regular spenders via phone, video chat, or email. If your customer base is too large for that approach, carve out a good sample size and get in touch to ask about their motivations and experiences.

IMPLEMENTING YOUR IDEAL CUSTOMER PROFILES

You might be wondering, "What if I have more than one ideal customer?" Many businesses do, and that is perfectly fine. You don't have to narrow everything down to a single ideal customer. But successful businesses tend to identify no more than three ideal customer profiles, and I encourage them not to go over that. Three profiles give you the flexibility to address multiple customer groups without diluting your messages too much. That said, I'd urge you to complete one ideal customer profile at a time in totality before moving on and tackling the next in the same way.

Every written communication you have with your prospects and clients should be consistent with their ideal customer profile and consider their past behaviors. Your copy should not sound like it was written by a soulless robot or a telemarketer. Tailor what you say and how you say it to meet the ideal customer where they are at that moment.

This means your marketing will be different for each of your ideal customer profiles. Why? Because they each have different objectives and pain points. By completing separate profiles for each ideal customer, you can approach them with the language and tone they need to hear to respond to your offer. Consider a tutoring center. The tone and content of communication best suited to get through to an ideal customer whose child is in danger of flunking out of school is going to sound very different from that suited to connect with an ideal customer whose child is trying to graduate in the top percentile of their class to get into their dream college.

To make all your ideal customer research worthwhile and effective, you must have a CRM system. It's a critical tool for survival. I don't care how big your tool is—if you're carrying around a machete or a pocketknife—this will be your single source of truth. The CRM is where the contact records for your customers—active, past, and prospective—are stored. This is where you're going to house information about them along the lines of "Loves chocolate ice cream, but don't send content about strawberry. He's allergic to it."

CRMs also make it easier to implement the rest of your Marketing RAMP. They will help you know who's buying and who's not, and where a customer is in the marketing process.[5] Since your CRM needs to be a power plant for the Marketing RAMP, you need reliable, consistent power. Getting your CRM up and running while building your Marketing RAMP is a perfect opportunity to save time, effort, and money.

LOVE SHOULD BE GIVEN AND RECEIVED

While the focus of this pillar is defining the people your business should love, keep in mind that the purpose of having a Marketing RAMP is to turn our love into a two-way street. You want your ideal customers to love you and your business just as much as you love them.

ALWAYS START WITH YOUR IDEAL CUSTOMER IN MIND

As a business owner or marketer, it's easy to forget that a normal person doesn't specifically dream about buying what it is you're selling. It's usually about something far deeper than the tangible good or service. It's about the promise that things are going to work out, that they are going to be loved, and that their life and the lives of their loved ones are going to turn out well.

Are the people buying perfume passionate about owning incredibly expensive scented water? No. They are investing in their goal to feel sexy, successful, and confident. If someone hires a realtor, do they simply need

---

5   If you're reading this and don't have a CRM for your business, or you have one that rarely is used, I've created a few resources to help you get that sorted out, which you can find at www.marketingbuiltbylove.com/crm.

someone to unlock the front door of their potential new home for them? No. They want a trusted advisor to help guide their decision and see them safely around unforeseen pitfalls and risks. There are elements of assurance, risk-avoidance, and aspiration in both examples.

In identifying whom you wish to love—your ideal customer—you have already made great headway in developing insights that will help you produce rich and valuable content for your marketing revamp. It is from the components of this profile (or profiles) that you will build out the communication, content, and entire experience of the Marketing RAMP. It is imperative that you know how to communicate with your ideal customers, and that is why we cover finding our love language in the next chapter.

TOP TAKEAWAYS

1. Identifying and fleshing out what your business's ideal customers look like is a step that most marketers fail to take seriously enough, and one that will pay dividends for the entire rest of the RAMP.

2. You can have more than one ideal customer profile, and your marketing should look different for each of them.

3. Understanding your ideal customer empowers you to speak directly to them about the pains and struggles in their life that your business can uniquely solve for them.

4. If you're unsure of who your ideal customers are, you don't need to do focus groups or conduct online surveys to identify them. Using the Pareto principle (the 80/20 rule), you'll be able to identify those who make up most of your revenue. Talking to them will provide invaluable insights into why they chose your business.

EXERCISE 1: YOUR IDEAL CUSTOMER

This is the first of fifteen exercises throughout this book that will help your business develop its own Marketing RAMP. You should complete them in numerical order since later exercises build on the answers to previous exercises.[6]

Use the following questions as your guide in fleshing out your profile of an ideal customer. This exercise is best done when you have the decision makers in your company together to provide their feedback. Not only will this help you and your colleagues get on the same page, but you'll also get the full picture from every department's perspective. We suggest you have leadership, marketing, sales, customer service, and fulfillment included when completing this section of the RAMP.

These lists outline the information you should identify for each of the four parts of an ideal customer profile:

- Demographics
  - Age
  - Gender
  - Marital status
  - Number of children
  - Child age range
  - Type of pets
  - Level of education
  - Ethnicity (if relevant)
  - Level of education
  - Annual household income
  - Whether they rent or own a home
  - Geographic location

---

6   You can document your answers however you like. You can also take advantage of the complimentary software we've developed at www.marketingramp.com.

- Interests
    - What do they want?
    - How do they perceive themselves?
    - What is their idea of success?
    - What do they value?
    - What prevents them from achieving what they want?
    - Where do they live online?
    - Who or what influences their decisions?
- Pain points—the challenges or problems the ideal customer encounters that your offering can solve (based on the answers to the following questions, define two to three pain points to feature in your communications)
    - Have they tried to fix this problem before and failed?
    - Did they have a bad experience with a competitor's solution?
    - How did these past unsuccessful efforts make them feel?
    - What objections to making a purchase do they have because of past experiences?
- Their relationship to you
    - What kinds of solutions are they looking for?
    - How will purchasing your product/service define them?
    - What business have they done with you in the past, if any?
    - Have they had interactions with your company but *not* made a purchase?

TIP: DEVELOP TWO OR THREE PROFILES

Few businesses have just *one* type of ideal customer. On the other hand, if you think you can serve "all customers," your business will be unfocused and unprofitable. You don't have to limit yourself to just one ideal customer profile, but I strongly urge you to define no more than two or three, especially at the start.

CHAPTER 4

RAMP Pillar 2: Our Love Language (the Brand Voice)

Once you know who your brand should fall in love with, you then must
develop the language to attract them to you.

THE RIGHT WORDS CHOSEN AND CRAFTED into a message can change the
world for the better.

If you've heard Martin Luther King Jr.'s "I Have a Dream" speech,
watched Ronald Reagan declare, "Mr. Gorbachev, tear down this wall,"
or listened to John F. Kennedy say that we choose to go to the moon not
because it is easy but because it is hard,[7] then you know exactly what I'm
talking about.

Each of these men uttered words that sparked hope around the world,
united nations, and galvanized men and women to take action toward a
better tomorrow that's full of promise. To become a powerful speaker, each

---

7   Martin Luther King Jr., "I Have a Dream" speech, August 28, 1963, https://www.marshall
    .edu/onemarshallu/i-have-a-dream; Ronald Reagan, address at the Brandenburg Gate, June
    12, 1987, https://www.archives.gov/publications/prologue/2007/summer/berlin.html; John
    F. Kennedy, address at Rice University, September 12, 1962, https://www.jfklibrary.org/
    archives/other-resources/john-f-kennedy-speeches/rice-university-19620912.

of these men had to know their audience and deliver their message in a way that would most likely connect with that target demographic. I can hear you asking, "What do these famous speeches have to do with marketing?"

If you think about what marketing is trying to achieve, then you will quickly realize the answer. We want to foster genuine connection with the listener, convince them to do what we ask of them, and use our powers of persuasion for the good of all parties involved. While it is crucial to have a developed understanding of who our ideal customers are, it is equally important to know how to talk to them most effectively. The right communication to the right audience will move them to action. The types of words uttered, the tonality they're spoken or written with, the empathy conveyed while doing so, and the level of complexity in the message must all be strategically selected. And that's why language is the second of the four pillars of the Marketing RAMP (see Figure 4.1).

If we get the balance right, we'll have a winning formula that moves the intended audience from an inactive state to an active state—the entire point of marketing. In this chapter, I talk generally about how all

Figure 4.1. The second pillar of the Marketing RAMP.

your marketing efforts should reflect the love language you want to speak to your ideal customer (this is the background you'll need to complete Exercise 2). In the next chapter, I dive into the details of how to shape a voice that your ideal customers will connect with.

WHAT IS A BRAND VOICE?

As a brand, we must speak the language of the people whom we wish to communicate with. It's imperative we come across as ordinary enough that what we say is relatable but extraordinary enough that we are seen as aspirational.

Martin Luther King Jr. had a distinct and powerful speaking voice that he developed over his time as a preacher, and it served him well in his famous speech. The cadence he employed to such great effect in this address is akin to the way he delivered his sermons from the pulpit. For his part, Ronald Reagan had experience as an actor. He knew how to compose himself for maximum impact, how to entertain by delivering a story we could follow, and how to sway people's emotions.

I'm not undermining the standalone value of their messages, but I am commending these men for understanding the art of communication. They knew how to speak the language of their audiences, meeting the two criteria I outlined above: ordinary enough that listeners could relate to them and extraordinary enough that people aspired to be like them and were open to their message. If they were marketers, we'd call this their *brand voice*.

In business, having an appropriate brand voice means using the words that our ideal customers use. We must speak how our customers speak, with the appropriate level of formality.

The brand voice underpins the entirety of a business's marketing communications. It is the electrical current that must run through all the content we put out, sparking an emotional response and galvanizing our prospects into action. If we use this knowledge with integrity, then we will wield robust marketing results.

You might have the most incredible product since sliced bread or the best service and customer-centric culture imaginable. But if you don't capture and communicate that in the right way, you will not achieve the results your company deserves.

If you get your brand voice wrong, it will alienate the people you're trying to reach. Think about it like this: I'm at a quantum physics convention, and I walk up to a group of Ivy League–educated physicists and say, "Hey, how's it hanging? Man, have you guys looked up at the stars lately? So crazy beautiful, huh? Who even knows what's up there?" Not only will I likely be shunned, but I will also probably agitate them because I am so obviously not speaking their language and have no reason to be there. I'm an imposter, an intruder, and a threat.

To develop an effective brand voice, you have to deeply understand your customers. Let's talk about how to get into the minds of our ideal customers.

CONNECTING TO CUSTOMERS: THE EMPATHY MAP

An *empathy map* is a powerful tool that can help guide us as we cultivate and communicate our company's brand voice. It provides a way to visualize how different segments of content can fit together under a unifying theme. It allows us to chart and study the complexities of our ideal customer's experience so we can use those pieces of aligned content throughout our marketing, sales, and communication strategies.

Imagine if we were sorting buckets of paint by their colors. Red hues in one area, blues in another, yellows in a third, and green in the fourth. Separated, we know what color palette we have to work with. Together, we have everything we need to paint a brilliant picture. The empathy map provides your copywriter with everything they need to paint your company's brilliant picture with words that will resonate with your ideal customers.

To develop an empathy map, you want to review the information you compiled about your ideal customer (Exercise 1). Then, fill in the

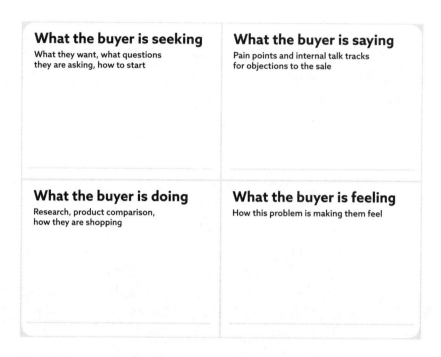

Figure 4.2. Four quadrants of an empathy map.

four quadrants of the empathy map (see Figure 4.2) by making your best guess at what your ideal customers are seeking, saying, doing, and feeling.

You'll find more information about how to complete an empathy map in Exercise 2. Doing the map helps your marketing efforts because you can snugly slot the relevant response into the messaging your company sends so that your selling point and stories become their stories. Your communication makes you part of their tribe and vice versa. We will do good business with those we align with and trust.

Figure 4.3 shows the empathy map for a luxury doggy day care and kennel company. They are positioning themselves as high-end doggy day care and want to appeal to high-end owners. (There is more on their story in Chapter 14 when I talk about customer delight.) Review the entries on the map, and then think about what you would say and how you would say it to connect with these buyers.

What the buyer is seeking	What the buyer is saying
What they want, what questions they are asking, how to start	Pain points and internal talk tracks for objections to the sale
Want to be assured that they are making the right choice for their pet. Asking questions about services, prices, and the environment their pet will encounter.	Statements about problems they've had finding good day care for their pet. Statments that reflect uncertainty, apprehension, worry, or nervousness, perhaps due to past experience with competitor.
What the buyer is doing	What the buyer is feeling
Research, product comparison, how they are shopping	How this problem is making them feel
Comparison with competitors; asking opinions of friends, vets, and pet professionals; looking up/reading reviews; looking at social pages and comments on socials; checking facility	Anxious and concerned about whether their dog is feeling happy; guilty for not being able to show their pet enough attention; at a loss for not knowing where to turn

Figure 4.3. Doggy day care empathy map.

HOW FORMAL SHOULD YOU BE?

I have a young son, and all you parents out there know that you don't speak to a young child the same way you do to your spouse. Teenagers often have their own language that excludes adults. All of us would not just dress differently but use a different tone of voice and different words when hanging with friends at a backyard barbecue versus going to a formal dinner.

The point is that we all instinctively know that we connect with other human beings using language, tone, and inflection, but this depends on the setting and audience. The same is true for our business communications, not just what happens in our personal lives.

Recently, I attended an event that featured a prominent author of a book that simplified accounting for business owners. The author had a packed room of eager learners.

At the beginning of his presentation, he spoke using simple words. He limited the amount of detail he went into so everyone could see the big picture. By using this approach, he was making a complex subject matter easy to understand. Everyone could follow what he was saying, and they were getting value from it. Everyone appreciated the presentation; the entire room was captivated.

During a short break, the room chattered in agreement about how amazing this presentation was and how the speaker was a financial genius. Many were already convinced they needed to hire him as a consultant.

What could go wrong?

After the break, he continued with his presentation, and this is where things went in a different direction. Rather than remembering who his audience was, he started talking at a level of detail and complexity that no one in the room could understand. He used industry terms and acronyms like "departmental LER ratios." He then started doing complex mathematical calculations step by step.

The room was so quiet that you could hear a pin drop.

A room full of people captivated by every word he spoke was now transformed into a room of people staring at their phones, answering emails, and scrolling through social media feeds.

He lost the room because he forgot the golden rule of communication: you must speak the language of the people whom you wish to communicate with. He went from speaking the language of the business owners in the audience—a language that they all knew—to the language of an expert accountant, which the audience did not speak.

As a brand, we must know how to speak the language of our ideal customers. Remember, it's imperative that we come across as ordinary enough that what we say is relatable but extraordinary enough that we are seen as aspirational.

Part of having a powerful, effective brand voice is using the words our customers use and speaking how our customers speak at their preferred level of formality. Think back to those great speeches I mentioned earlier, including MLK's "I Have a Dream," Ronald Reagan's "Tear down this wall," and JFK's speech about going to the moon. If you've never heard those speeches, find them on YouTube. Pay attention to the tone of voice that MLK, Ronald Reagan, and JFK used. Pay attention to the actual words they spoke and the inflections they chose. It was not by accident; all of this was carefully chosen to move the masses to action and get people behind their bold vision.

For example, take JFK's statement, "We choose to go to the moon in this decade and do the other things, not because they are easy but because they are hard."[8] Now, imagine hearing any other president say those words: Donald Trump, Barack Obama, Bill Clinton, or Joe Biden. With each president, the phrase would come across very differently because some of these people are much more formal than others. This is a perfect example of how changing your brand's spectrum of formality will completely change who listens, who is attracted to that message, and who is moved to action.

That's why another key step in defining your brand voice is to identify where you want to fall along what I call the *spectrum of formality* (see Figure 4.4). For each of the following four scales represented, identify where along the spectrum you should fall in terms of work selection, tone, and even images to best connect with your ideal customer:

- Casual or formal: "Hey, buddy, whatsup?" versus "Hello, Mrs. X. I hope you are well."

- Humorous or serious: "Our kayaks will slide through rapids like a pig at a mud-wrestling contest" versus "Our kayaks show remarkable maneuverability."

- Irreverent or respectful: "To that, we say, 'Okay, Boomer!'" versus "To that, the only response is that we need to get all the facts."

- Enthusiastic or matter-of-fact: "Our service will knock your socks off!" versus "We focus on exceeding customer expectations."

---

8   Kennedy, address at Rice University.

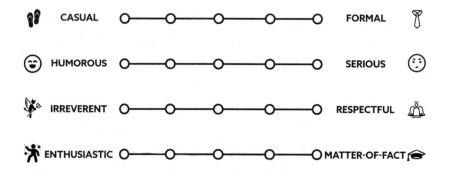

Figure 4.4. The spectrum of formality.

Here are some examples of the four scales:

- Your local burger joint's spectrum of formality will be much more *casual* versus having dinner at your city's Michelin-star restaurant, which will be more *formal*, on the opposite end of the burger stand's casual tone.

- Attending a comedy show, you'll experience a *humorous* spectrum of formality compared to sitting in a *serious* graduate-level presentation on microbiology by the resident professor emeritus at the local university.

- Imagine being transported back to the 1980s in New York and finding yourself in the famous CBGB, witnessing the iconic punk rock band the Sex Pistols belting out their lyrics to "Anarchy in the UK." Their spectrum of formality is absolutely on the side of *irreverent* and rebellious. Now, if you were whisked away to President Barack Obama's inauguration and witnessed Beyonce singing the U.S. National Anthem, you'd be hearing a *respectful* spectrum of formality.

- If you've ever watched a toddler open presents on Christmas morning, you have heard an *enthusiastic* spectrum of formality. And if you've ever been unfortunate enough to be pulled over by a police officer for speeding, you have likely heard a *matter-of-fact* spectrum of formality.

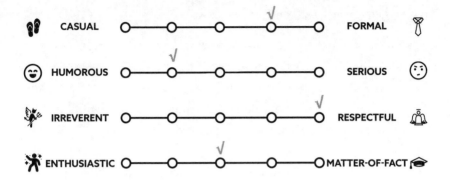

Figure 4.5. The spectrum of formality for the doggy day care.

Decisions about what level of formality you should use need to be clearly communicated to anyone writing copy or designing ads. The doggy day care company, for example, decided they want to be formal and respectful but also humorous and in the middle between enthusiastic and matter-of-fact (see Figure 4.5).

DEFINING YOUR BRAND VOICE

Having an empathy map creates the backdrop for defining your *brand voice*, the language, messages, and themes that should appear consistently in all your communications with prospects and customers. What follows is an overview of the four components you'll need to address (see Figure 4.6). Use Exercise 2, at the end of this chapter, and Exercise 3, at the end of the next chapter, to help you develop your own versions.

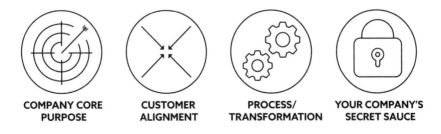

Figure 4.6. Four parts of the complete brand voice.

Define Your Company's Core Purpose

Traditional company core purposes have been bastardized: "We will provide value for our customer by delivering best-in-class . . . blah blah blah." Because the purpose is so generic, few people inside the company care about it or try to live out the values represented by the purpose.

To have a powerful brand voice, you need a core purpose that gets to the root of what you are really trying to do, which is attacking a great wrong, an injustice in the world that affects your ideal customers. (I call this the Great Travesty, and you'll find more about how to define this for your organization in Chapter 8.) Your mission, your core purpose for being in business, is to stop the injustice in its tracks and rid the world of it. Or at least make the situation much more bearable for customers.

This modern-day version of a purpose is much more actionable and allows everyone—staff, vendors, and customers—to get behind it. Plus, it's authentic, and we can clearly see how or if our company is resolving the customer's biggest challenge or frustration. To define this purpose, you will need to answer five questions:

- What does your company do?
- Why is it important to the world or at least to your customers?
- Why does this matter?
- What was the founder's passion or purpose in starting the company?
- What do you want to be known for?

Customer Alignment

Ensure that your products and services are aligned with the customer's values and pain points. To create this alignment, start by thinking about the values you and your ideal customers share:

- What do your customers value?
- How do your company's philosophy and offerings align with those values?

Then, evaluate this information in light of your description of an ideal customer (their pain points, objections, concerns, prior failures, etc.). In other words, what does your company do and how do you do it, and how does that reflect your values and match up with customers' values? From a marketing perspective, how can you shape your customer communications to make this alignment obvious to the prospect?

PROVIDING VALUE-ADDED CONTENT TO SUPPORT THE CUSTOMER'S JOURNEY

Before a customer makes a significant purchasing decision, they will consume some type of content. For example, when you enter a restaurant, you will read the menu before you make your purchase decision (order). Before you buy a new computer, refrigerator, car, or home, you'll consume some type of content—research, reviews, articles—so you feel best informed on your decision.

One way to manifest your alignment with your ideal customers is to figure out what content will help them make a faster, better (more informed) purchasing decision. Then make sure you provide it for them, so they don't have to work as hard in making their decision. You can actually speed up their time to purchase as well as create rapport by guiding them with valuable info that helps them make their decision. Do this with integrity, and you will be positioned to win the sale and beat your competition every time.

Process (Steps to Success)

At its simplest, the process of converting a prospect into a happy customer has just three steps:

1. What steps you want them to take (including the primary call to action)

2. What they'll experience during that process

3. The success they'll have once they are using your product or service

Here are two examples of this process for achieving success:

- Example 1: A company that sells instructional software

  1. Speak with our consultant: Schedule a call with a team member to learn about what we offer and the process that makes student success possible.

  2. Launch our solution: Put your customized program into action and benefit from personalized educator development and resources.

  3. Celebrate happier teachers and engaged students: Watch as your student culture transforms, bringing about happier teachers and elevating student success.

- Example 2: A company that sells strategic business and personal planning services

  1. Schedule a free personal consultation: Click the button to get in touch for a free consultation.

  2. Get a smart and easy-to-understand plan: Our experienced team provides clarity and lays out a plan to reach your goals.

  3. Stop worrying and start living: Feel the joy and comfort of being on a path toward your business or life goals.

You'll need to flesh out these steps in more detail once you get to Pillar 4, but for the purpose of shaping your marketing communications, it's great if you can distill the entire process into three simple steps that succinctly—in three short sentences—explain to your ideal customers how they can do business with you.

Your Secret Sauce

Your brand voice must consistently reflect the two or three things your company does better than the competition. This is what sets you apart. I call this your *secret sauce*, and I go into more depth in the next chapter about how to define it.

SPEAKING DIRECTLY TO YOUR IDEAL CUSTOMERS

Pillar 2 of the Marketing RAMP lays the foundation for all the communications you will use when dealing with customers. It tells you what kinds of language and images you need to feature so that your ideal customers will quickly recognize your company's offer as something that matches their needs, pain points, interests, and values.

 ## TOP TAKEAWAYS

1. If you're not careful to speak the language of the people you're selling to, your business will never reach the level of success it's capable of, regardless of the quality of your brand.

2. It's not only about getting the tone, word choice, and formality right but also about communicating the heart of your business in the form of an easily digestible story.

3. Understanding how the human brain works and how your messaging will be processed by your target audience is crucial to truly be heard by them.

EXERCISE 2: YOUR BRAND VOICE, PART 1

This exercise will help you get started on developing a brand voice. The next chapter and Exercise 3 go into more depth about the final element, the secret sauce.

This exercise is best done when you have the decision makers in your company together to provide their feedback. Not only will this help you and your colleagues get on the same page, but also, you'll get the full picture from every department's perspective. We suggest you have leadership, marketing, sales, customer service, and fulfillment included when completing this section of the RAMP.

TIP: THIS IS A FIRST PASS!

Everything you define here will likely become clearer as you work through the other components of RAMP. For now, use whatever existing information you have and take your best guess at answers. Then, know that you'll want to come back and refine the voice later on. After you've done more work around that, it will help you clarify components such as how to explain your company's purpose and how to understand your customer's pain points and needs.

Develop an Empathy Map

Review the information you've compiled about your customers, and then populate the four quadrants of an empathy map (Figure 4.2) by answering the following questions:

1. What the buyer is *seeking*:
    -   What are they looking for, both literally and emotionally?
    -   What questions are they asking themselves before they buy?
    -   How do they go about pursuing what it is they want?

2. What the buyer is *saying*:

    - What are the pain points the customer wants alleviated?

    - What is their internal talk track saying about the solution you're offering?

    - Why might they be internally objecting to the sale?

3. What the buyer is *doing*:

    - What research are they undertaking before the moment of decision?

    - What other products in the market are they comparing yours to?

    - What is the medium through which they are shopping?

4. What the buyer is *feeling*:

    - How is this problem making them feel?

    - Are they hopeful your solution might help them?

    - How do their feelings align or clash with what they are saying?

Identify the Level of Formality

1. Have your team talk about each of the four scales that make up the spectrum of formality (Figure 4.4) and identify where along those scales you want to fall.

2. For each scale, develop example statements that illustrate acceptable language versus unacceptable language and tone. (This will help future writings meet the targets.)

Define How You Align with Your Customers

Review what your customers value, their pain points, objections to the sale, any prior experiences they've had, and how this aligns with your company. What you do and say and how you use your words assures customers that doing business with you is the right choice. Identify the following points:

- Your customer's values

- How your company aligns with their values

Define the Steps to Success

What are the three simple steps that customers will take in doing business with you? Your version should describe the following:

- What you want them to do; this usually includes the primary call to action

- What they'll experience or get during that process

- The success they'll have once they have finished consuming your product or service

Identify or Develop Value-Added Content and Social Proof

Think for a moment about what kind of content your ideal customers are already consuming or will likely consume before they make their purchasing decision. The more complex and expensive your product or service is, the higher the likelihood that they'll need more content for them to consume before they buy. What content should you be providing along their customer journey to change them from a prospect into a customer?

Content considerations include the following:

- Product or service education

- Product or service comparison

- Product or service features tied to benefits

Also, review the social proof you're collecting and the testimonials you have, and gather together or flag those that most clearly express your brand voice. Make sure they are linked to the brand voice section of your Marketing RAMP so that you can easily locate them later.

CHAPTER 5

Your Company's Secret Sauce

Every superhero has a superpower that makes them
invincible. Your business has a superpower, and that unique
power must be baked into your very own secret sauce.

INSIDE A HEAVILY SECURED MUSEUM IN Atlanta, Georgia, there is a high-tech bank vault that can withstand any type of firepower. In there rests the secret recipe for Coca-Cola. For many multibillion-dollar brands like Coke, much of their success lies in understanding, protecting, and promoting the immense value of their unique traits, what I call the *secret sauce*.

Every business should define its secret sauce—the special aspects of its products or services that people are going to remember about their brand over everything else.

Why is this work important? The human brain is overwhelmed with four hundred billion bits of information per second, all competing for its attention. As incredible as the human brain is, there's simply too much information and stimuli competing for its attention. Therefore, the brain filters nearly all of it so that the conscious mind is only aware of roughly two thousand out of the four hundred billion bits of information flowing in.[9]

---

9   Joe Dispenza, *Evolve Your Brain: The Science of Changing Your Mind* (Deerfield Beach, FL: Health Communications, 2008).

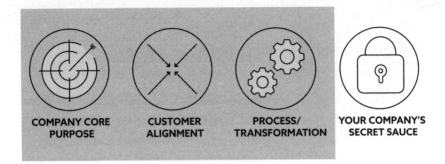

Figure 5.1. The secret sauce component of a brand voice.

Every successful company knows how to use its secret sauce to its advantage throughout sales, marketing, and line extensions. You must ensure that your brand and your message is top of mind for your ideal customers. Featuring your secret sauce will help you get to the front of the line. Your secret sauce, when well executed, will make your product or service so unique that it stands out above and beyond your competition, and it will motivate your customers to talk about your company with their friends, family, and colleagues.

That's why, among the four parts of brand voice (see Figure 5.1), determining your secret sauce deserves special attention. This chapter and Exercise 3 will help you identify your company's own secret sauce.

PICK THREE: INGREDIENTS FOR A SECRET SAUCE

I live in San Diego, and I am spoiled with choices when it comes to good fish tacos. However, despite the many tasty options, there is one restaurant I am fiercely loyal to. I have become addicted to their secret sauce, you could say. There are six potential ingredients that go into determining a secret sauce:

1. *Time:* When can your customers expect to see results?

2. *Price:* How does the price of your product measure up to your competitors?

3. *Unique features:* What about your product makes it special?

4. *Innovation:* What about the experience you provide your customers is creative?

5. *Experience:* Is the process enjoyable for the customers who buy from you?

6. *Success:* How does your product or service benefit the customer?

Any given recipe should have no more than three ingredients. Even in the fictional world of superheroes, no one hero possessed all the powers. Each hero had only a select few that made them truly great. The same case must be made for your business, too.

As you embark on Exercise 3 (which will help you identify your company's secret sauce), keep in mind that you can't be truly great at everything. You can have no more than three of the six, and many businesses have less than three. How your ingredients meld together is what will set your business apart from the rest.

Back to my taco stand. Does it have ocean views? No. Do they play good music? No. But that's okay. That's not what I'm there for. What they do have is a lot of unique features: incredibly fresh seafood (caught that day and displayed on ice) and a variety of marinades (each as good as the last). They also offer a great experience. They have the perfect ambiance that's casual enough that I can walk in with my flip-flops but nice enough that I enjoy getting a beer and hanging around while I eat my tacos. They're not the best at everything. But, as far as I'm concerned, nailing two secret sauce ingredients—features and experience—is enough to keep me going back. And I will keep telling my friends to give it a try.

Let's consider Amazon's ecommerce business through this lens of secret sauce ingredients. If we were to identify the parts of their secret sauce, what would we choose?

1. Time: They've got free two-day or sometimes even same-day delivery. Yes, this is a superpower of theirs.

2. Price: They offer a range of similar products at different price points, many of them the cheapest available on the market. Yes, price is a superpower.

3. Unique features: They have an incredibly wide variety of products. Yes, I'd argue this is their final superpower.

4. Innovation: While their speedy delivery times and free shipping used to be novel, this has largely become the norm across internet retailers. So, no, not an ingredient of their secret sauce.

5. Experience: Their website is not beautiful; nor is the experience of unboxing the products especially remarkable. This is a no.

6. Success: Are they delivering success to you? Not in any noteworthy way.

As you work to identify the secret sauce for your own business, remember to choose no more than three elements to emphasize. As you see here, even one of the most successful companies in the world does not shine across every category. That's not the goal. Instead, if you're committed to remaining great at what you want to be great at and you know how to communicate to your ideal customers what makes you so uniquely great, then you're set.

TIP: WHAT INGREDIENTS ARE YOUR COMPETITORS EMPHASIZING?

Once you have settled on your strengths, it would be wise to review your top two competitors and examine what you think their superpowers are. This is something I always find value in when looking at it from the angle of how we'll be communicating our secret sauce to the world. This knowledge can be used not only in crafting your brand pitch, as I discuss in the next chapter, but in subsequent communications across several stages in the customer journey, which I address in Parts II and III.

GETTING PAST THE REPTILIAN BRAIN

Once you know what your secret sauce is, you need to get its distinct taste into all your communications. That's what will help you break through the brain's gatekeeper in the reptilian brain. If the ancient reptilian brain says, "This will help me survive," the next-level mammalian brain is free to add, "This makes me feel good." The largest portion of our brain—the neocortex, or logical brain, which is where complex thought happens—then kicks in. It can evaluate information rationally because it deals with numbers, forecasting, deductive reasoning, and logic.

Even for people who believe they are rational and unswayed by appeals to emotion, the final buying decision can only be made in the logical brain with the reptilian and mammalian brains' permission. It's fascinating to understand this. That's likely why researchers continue to conduct studies on humans, primates, mammals, and even some breeds of birds to see how their brains respond to the offer of a small reward instantly versus a delayed reward that is greater and requires patience and forethought.

How does this link to marketing messages? Once the prospect's reptilian brain buys into my proposition and concludes that what I'm trying to convey has survival value, it then passes the message to that person's mammalian brain, which handles feelings. At this point, the brain releases a chemical called oxytocin. Oxytocin signals that this message is important, and we should pay attention. We have now chemically engaged their mind and body.

At this crucial juncture, we must make sure that we're connecting with them emotionally. You want your customer to feel like you understand their struggles, that you've been there before yourself. That's why you're offering a solution—you truly get their pain.

Oxytocin isn't the only chemical at play. Our bodies release dopamine when we experience pleasure. Dopamine is also the chemical associated with reward. Humans are hardwired to enjoy dopamine. Whether consciously or not, people are constantly seeking out their next dopamine hit. Everything from social media scrolling to video games to illegal drugs has been designed to trigger dopamine release to keep users coming back for more. Ever find yourself mindlessly scrolling and scrolling through some social media feed and suddenly you come back to yourself and wonder why? That's your brain seeking another dopamine hit, convinced it might be hiding just beyond the next scroll.

As marketers, we often try to trigger this response. Why? If what we're selling is identified with pleasure, our chances of making a sale go way up. We certainly do not want to take advantage of people's emotions or weaponize their internal chemical responses, but we absolutely do want customers to fall in love with our brand.

Think about the number of car commercials that highlight stunning landscapes and American ideals. It's not a thorough description of features and benefits that sells something. It's the story and the emotions you feel from it that are so compelling.

Consider the way athletic wear companies emphasize overcoming the odds and hard work. A young man might watch their commercial and feel excited and inspired to buy the brand's products. He wants to tap into the inspiration he just saw on the screen. The logical brain then kicks in and calls for a visit to the local store to try on some of the brand's apparel and see if it fits and looks like what he's seen on TV. There, he will evaluate not only the look and feel but also the cost. Is what he'd be getting worth what he'd have to pay? If the marketing was done well, his perception of wearing the brand—the aspirational pursuit to elevate his status whether physically, socially, or emotionally—should create more upside than the price he'll pay.

SPICING UP SOCIAL PROOF WITH YOUR SECRET SAUCE

The human brain is wired to ensure your survival. Stepping into the unknown is a risk; danger could lurk around any corner. With the way the human brain is wired, it feels better to stay in one's current state of known pain rather than opting into an unknown state that could bring even greater pain and risk.

These internal objections are what will prevent your ideal customers from buying from you—that is, until the Marketing RAMP helps you address each pain point one by one to remove hesitation and pave the path to a purchase.

That's why it's important to get potential customers the information they need to have, providing it in story form and from a source that (after all your hard work) your prospects perceive to be like them. You aren't selling to them in a way that's off-putting, and you aren't giving them boring, generic case studies. Instead, you have done your due diligence in identifying and studying your ideal customer. You know their pain points, and you understand what internal objections could crop up and how those concerns dictate the stories you want these testimonials to tell. You should have one story prepared for each ideal customer type, and you should have your secret sauce on hand to sprinkle liberally throughout the story assembly process.

Let's use a gym as an example. The owner knows that people come to his gym for one or more of the following three reasons:

1. To lose weight

2. To gain strength (muscle mass)

3. To improve their health

How can the gym connect with these ideal customers? Think about the internal voice of a person who has tried and failed at weight loss. It might sound like this: *Remember the last time you tried to lose weight? It didn't work out. You wasted time and money on that personal trainer and gym membership because you never even went. Maybe this is just the way I am. This is how my body is built. It's silly for me to think I can change that. I need to focus on other things like my family and not myself.*

If we do the same for the other two types of potential customers, what emerge are three distinct lines of communication:

1. "You want to lose weight but never found anything that worked for you."

2. "You want to gain muscle mass, and you've tried everything but aren't seeing results."

3. "You want to improve your health, so you'll have more energy, but all the cleanses in the world haven't helped."

The next step for the gym owner is to develop a success story around each of these messages. All three will highlight why his gym is uniquely suited to best meet an ideal customer's needs. (See Chapter 8 for more about success stories.)

YOUR SECRET SAUCE IS A POWERFUL TOOL

As marketers, everything we do must take into account how human brains process information. Nearly everyone makes their initial decision based on emotion and then reinforces or rejects that initial conclusion through logic. This means that, while it's an incredibly valuable part of our Marketing RAMP assembly, we cannot rely on our secret sauce alone. Nonetheless, understanding the reptilian brain and the fact that decisions are driven by emotions first and seeing how the secret sauce can be used to get our brand's messaging to the next part of the brain work together to give us the highest likelihood of turning our prospects into our customers.

Once you and your team have found what makes you special, the next action is to present this proposal to the world of people you love—your ideal customers. We master this art form in the next chapter as we dive deep into the brand pitch.

 TOP TAKEAWAYS

1. You don't have to be the best at everything. You just need to be unique and make sure your customers know—and remember—that you're giving them something no one else can.

2. Your secret sauce should have no more than three ingredients of the six possible categories.

3. Once you figure out what your unique point of difference is, it should be present in every communication you're sending out.

4. Once you've figured out your company's secret sauce, it is wise to choose your top two competitors and do the same exercise. This will provide you with an understanding of where your company outshines the competition, which can be used in your marketing, sales, and communications.

5. While we never want to manipulate people's emotions with ill intent, it's necessary to engage our prospects' emotions through our marketing efforts, triggering a pleasure response as often as possible.

EXERCISE 3: YOUR BRAND VOICE, PART 2

Here are the questions used for determining your company's secret sauce that will help you shape your brand voice. This exercise is best done when you have the decision makers in your company together to provide their feedback. Not only will this help you and your colleagues get on the same page, but you'll also get the full picture from every department's perspective. We suggest you have leadership, marketing, sales, customer service, and fulfillment included when completing this section of the RAMP.

Identify the Ingredients

Identify no more than three of the areas where your company shines brightest from the list below.

1. Time: When can your customers expect to see results?

2. Price: How does the price of your product measure up to your competitors?

3. Unique features: What about your product makes it special?

4. Innovation: What about the experience you provide your customers is creative?

5. Experience: Is the process enjoyable for customers who buy from you?

6. Success: How does your product or service benefit the customer?

Compare Your Sauce to the Competition

Once you've identified your company's secret sauce, it is worthwhile choosing your top two competitors and doing a side-by-side comparison. Create a three-column sheet on which you will enter information about your ingredients and those of your competitors.[10] This will give you a powerful visual of where your company stands in comparison to your toughest competition.

---

10 You can, of course, use our free software (www.marketingramp.com), in which we have created templates for you to use and share with your colleagues.

CHAPTER 6

RAMP Pillar 3: Our Proposal (the Brand Pitch)

*If you want the person you love (your ideal customer)
to commit to you, you must have a well-thought-out
proposal ready to use at the right time.*

HAVE YOU EVER TURNED OFF OR walked out of a movie that failed to keep your interest? Maybe the film had underdeveloped characters. Maybe the risk-reward dynamic wasn't clear, or the action wasn't compelling. Perhaps the storyline fell flat, with the characters saying the wrong things at the wrong times. You realized you really didn't care how it ended; it wasn't worth your time.

This is the same fate too many marketers succumb to. They make the wrong move and ruin what could be a magical moment where the person they love, their ideal customer, says "yes" and commits to a purchase. By not carefully crafting the entire experience and conveying the right thing at the right time, engagement plummets and the connection is lost. This means that once you find your brand voice and get your message's tone and content just right, it's equally important to figure out how to deliver it most effectively.

Figure 6.1. The third pillar of the Marketing RAMP.

Because human beings' attention spans are short and the average person is exposed to six thousand ads per day, you need to craft a message that will break through the onslaught and get people's attention fast, motivating them to take action.[11] Essentially, you must distill the entirety of your brand voice into a tight, highly effective *brand pitch*, which is the core element of the third pillar of the Marketing RAMP, our proposal (see Figure 6.1). How to craft a targeted brand pitch is the topic of this chapter and Exercise 4.

WHAT IS A BRAND PITCH?

A brand pitch is a well-crafted and succinct explanation of what you do, whom you do it for, and why you are better than your competition. Clear, concise communication is the key to attracting prospects and

---

11 Louise Story, "Anywhere the Eye Can See, It's Likely to See an Ad," *New York Times*, January 1, 2015, https://www.nytimes.com/2007/01/15/business/media/15everywhere.html.

converting them into customers. In other words, the brand pitch should be designed to appeal primarily to the reptilian brain. Why? Because in thirty seconds, all you can do is make it past the brain's gatekeeper and, hopefully, get a good response from the mammalian brain.

The brand pitch is catered to people who haven't bought from you yet and maybe have never even heard of your company. In just a few sentences, you want to communicate what it is you do and what makes you better than the competition. Another benefit of having distilled your secret sauce recipe is that it can help you understand where your competitors are strong and where they are weak. It's a simplified version of a SWOT (strengths, weaknesses, opportunities, and threats) analysis, and it can be used to tailor your messaging around how you are the better option. It can also be used to inform your strategies in future sales and marketing initiatives, helping you go on the offense to acquire competitors' customers.

This doesn't have to be direct or resemble a smear campaign, but if you don't address why you're better than the competition, your customer is going to decide for themselves. Or worse, the competition will tell them why they're better than you. So, with integrity and respect, you need to communicate your secret sauce.

The brand pitch can be used:

- To ensure your employees are united in their understanding of your mission

- By your sales team

- In your marketing communications

- On your website and in your collateral

- In casual conversations

THE BRAND PITCH FORMULA

The brand pitch formula is made up of six parts, as shown in Figure 6.2:

1. *We are*, which describes the nature of your business

2. *We serve*, which is the label you assign to your ideal customers

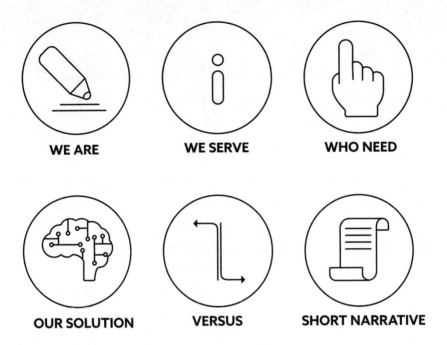

WE ARE   **WE SERVE**   **WHO NEED**

OUR SOLUTION   **VERSUS**   **SHORT NARRATIVE**

Figure 6.2. The brand pitch formula.

3. *Who need*, which describes the ideal customer's pain point

4. *Our solution*, which describes how your business eliminates the pain

5. *Versus*, which describes why your solution is different from alternative solutions

6. *Short narrative*, which summarizes all the above points in story form

Exercise 4 walks you through the steps of creating your own brand pitch. But first, let's look at each of the components in more detail.

We Are

To generate your "We Are" statement, start by writing down your company name and then, using fewer than ten words, add a short description of what your company does. You might be tempted to add unnecessary descriptive words, but avoid doing this. Keep it simple and to the point.

Using my business as an example, I'd say: *Built by Love is a digital marketing agency.*

We Serve

To create the "We Serve" statement, describe who your ideal customer is in ten words or fewer. The more precise you can be with whom you serve, the better. Remember when we worked through your ideal customers? We talked about how it would be wonderful if everyone was your customer. But that cannot be the reality right now, and we need a succinct and focused audience. We can put that to use here and call out your ideal customers in this statement.

Continuing using Built by Love as an example, the "We Serve" statement would be: *Businesses who want to improve the world, make a profit, and be market leaders.*

You might be wondering why my example above is broad when I told you to be narrow and focused. My agency is focused on serving business owners who truly want to make the world a better place, and they need a proven way to get their product out in the world to help as many people as possible. You're about to see how it all comes together in the next part, "Who Need."

Who Need

The "Who Need" statement summarizes your ideal customer's primary pain point. Or it is a tightly worded amalgamation of the top several relevant pain points.

Following our working example, Built by Love's "Who Need" statement is: *A proven marketing system that consistently delivers a return on its investment, producing leads, value to customers, and new sales.*

As a word of advice for crafting your own "Who Need" statement, many people at this point start talking about the solution rather than the problem. The solution is our next statement. This one must be the pain agitator.

Our Solution

The "Our Solution" statement communicates how your company can fill the defined needs of the previous pain point.

Built by Love's "Our Solution" statement is: *The Marketing RAMP is a foundational plan that delivers consistent marketing results, harnessing the power of how the human brain processes information, the science behind human relationships, and the stages of the buyer's journey.*

You'll notice this example is a bit long, and that's perfectly all right if you have developed a statement that you feel strongly about. The statements that we're crafting in these steps will eventually be pieced together to form your master brand pitch. Further tightening can be done at that point.

Versus

The "Versus" statement is where you differentiate yourself from the competition. Here you address your competitors, not by their name but by the weaknesses or inferiority of their solutions, their process, or their results. It's important not to go on the attack but rather to illuminate how what you're doing is different from what others are offering. And not only different—better.

This part of the brand pitch is often the most challenging. I suggest reviewing your secret sauce decisions. In establishing that recipe, you already identified your company's strengths, as well as how they stack up to your competitors' strengths. This is an ideal place to draw from as you craft your "Versus" statement.

Going back to our Built by Love example: *Outdated marketing funnels focus on short-term results rather than long-term customer growth; these tactics produce poor customer experiences, leak repeat purchase opportunities, and do more damage than good.*

Notice, in the example provided, that we attacked the entire marketing industry rather than comparing our agency's strengths to another agency's weaknesses. This is a useful example because it shows how to use this statement to separate your company from the entire industry, and that's precisely what we did here. The "Versus" statement also must complement and be aligned with a theme I call the Great Travesty, which I teach you about in Chapter 8.

Brand Narrative

Now it's time to assemble the five parts in sequential order. You'll need to make a few simple adjustments to turn the statements into flowing sentences. Consider how the example I've been using comes together:

> Built by Love is a digital marketing agency *serving* businesses who want to improve the world, make a profit, and be market leaders and *who need* a proven marketing system that consistently delivers a return on its investment, producing leads, value to customers, and new sales. *Our solution* is the Marketing RAMP, a foundational plan that delivers consistent marketing results by harnessing the power of how the human brain processes information, the science behind human relationships, and the critical stages of the buyer's journey, *versus* outdated marketing funnels that focus on short-term results rather than long-term customer growth. These tactics produce poor customer experiences, leak repeat purchase opportunities, and do more damage than good.

POLISHING YOUR PITCH

While this version of my company's brand pitch isn't bad, it's still too long for effective communication with someone who is unfamiliar with my company. That's true of most brand pitches I've seen. So you're not done until you polish the first draft. I advise condensing a brand pitch into sixty words or fewer, with unnecessary words eliminated. Here's a fifty-four-word version of my company's brand pitch, less than half the original length:

> Built by Love is a digital marketing agency *serving* businesses who want to be market leaders *who need* a marketing strategy that delivers a return on its investment. *Our solution* is the Marketing RAMP, a foundational plan that delivers consistent results by harnessing the power of neuroscience, evolution of relationships, and the buyer's journey.

If you need an even tighter version, you can continue to knock out what isn't essential until you are left with the simplest sentence possible. At Built by Love, we could get that down to: *We help small businesses improve their marketing with our proprietary Marketing RAMP.* When you read that, you know that you're either in the right place or you're not. We might already have gotten through your reptilian brain.

USING YOUR BRAND PITCH

The brand pitch should always be in mind when you introduce a prospect to your business. While it can inform future marketing campaigns generally, it can also be put to direct use across your enterprise from the moment it's crafted. It can be used in advertising copy, in sales, on social media, and even be featured on your website.

If it isn't clear already, I'll say it explicitly: the final copy of your brand pitch is of the utmost importance. Often, business owners decide to tackle this themselves. I don't doubt there are business owners who are both great at what they do in their business and also top-tier copywriters. But that is the exception and not the rule. Additionally, the shortest copy is almost always the most challenging to write well. Given the importance of an airtight brand pitch—and the way in which the brand voice is intended to unify the tonality and approach you employ as you interact with your ideal customer multiple times and in multiple forms throughout the Marketing RAMP process—this may be the time to bring in professional marketing assistance.

That said, like all marketing communications, your brand pitch does not need to be perfect and concrete. This is a living, breathing communication tool that should evolve over time. Having a "version one" is much better than having a "version none," as it sets you up to confidently and warmly welcome people onto the customer journey that you have built especially for them.

TIP: UPDATE YOUR "ABOUT US" WEB PAGE

Your brand pitch can revolutionize the often mishandled "About Us" page. Very few people connect with a historical account of where your brand started. They're not interested in grainy pictures of the founder or new images of the office space full of happy, coffee-drinking employees. They want a story, and they want to know what you have to offer them. If you still want to add in, "We've been fortunate to help transform people's lives since 1998, and here's our team of people" at the end and get that grainy picture up there, that's fine. But without communicating the direct value of what you do through your brand pitch somewhere on there, your "About Us" page is being wasted. The core of what your business is about should be your customers, not you.

TOP TAKEAWAYS

1. You need to be able to communicate in a clear and concise manner what you do, whom you do it for, and why your solution is the best available, or else your prospects' brains will refuse to retain your messaging.

2. Your brand pitch is focused on communicating with ideal customers who have never purchased from you before, also referred to as "prospects" in the world of sales.

3. In a respectful and professional manner, your brand pitch needs to address why you're better than the competition, or your competition will tell your prospective customers why they're better than you.

4. It's worth putting in the time to get your brand pitch just right because its uses across your business are varied and powerful. If you find yourself hung up on words within your brand pitch, remember that "version one" is always better than "version none." You can always update, improve, and polish later.

5. The brand pitch should be used across your sales and marketing communications. It should live on your website, and one of the perfect places to put the entire brand pitch is your "About Us" section.

EXERCISE 4: YOUR BRAND PITCH

Here are the questions used for determining your company's brand pitch. I suggest you have leadership from marketing, sales, customer service, and fulfillment participate. Not only will this help you and your colleagues get on the same page, but you'll also get the full picture from every department's perspective.

We Are

To generate your "We Are" statement, start by writing down your company name and then—using fewer than ten words—add a short description of what your company does.

We Serve

To create the "We Serve" statement, describe who your ideal customer is in ten words or fewer.

Who Need

The "Who Need" statement summarizes your ideal customer's primary pain point or else is a tightly worded amalgamation of several top relevant pain points.

Our Solution

The "Our Solution" statement communicates how your company can fill the defined needs of the previous pain point.

Versus

The "Versus" statement is where we differentiate ourselves from the competition. Here we address our competitors, not by their name, but by the weaknesses or inferiority of their solutions, their process, or their results.

Brand Narrative

Now it's time to assemble the five parts in sequential order. You'll need to make a few simple adjustments to turn the statements into flowing sentences.

CHAPTER 7

RAMP Pillar 4: The Relationship Journey

The fourth and final pillar of the RAMP is composed of ten stages covering the buyer's journey. These define how you will implement the RAMP in your marketing department.

WHEN I WAS SIXTEEN YEARS OLD, my family pooled together the money they had to buy me a green 1968 Volkswagen Beetle. To me, that little green Bug represented freedom—freedom to go where I wanted without having to rely on others. And yet, as much as I loved my car, I quickly learned how unreliable it was. After breaking down on me for the dozenth time, I decided I'd had enough.

I bought a book called *How to Keep Your Volkswagen Alive: A Manual of Step-by-Step Procedures for the Complete Idiot.* Over a three-month span, I removed every single part of the engine piece by piece and then put it back together again, hoping for a better outcome. I held my breath, but when I stuck the key in and the ignition turned over, the engine didn't rumble to life. Instead, there was deafening silence and a sense of defeat. I wanted to bang my head on the steering wheel.

As my VW Bug did, the Marketing RAMP should bring you a

sense of freedom. But unlike my initially ineffective mechanic work at sixteen, I don't want you to hold the uncomfortable doubt that the RAMP might fail to work when you deploy it, even during the process of building the RAMP. That's why this chapter concisely outlines how the fourth pillar needs to be structured. The other three pillars form the foundation of this last and final one. It's the piece of the process that forms the engine, powering you toward freedom and away from failed marketing and lackluster sales.

By this point in the foundational marketing constructing process, you have articulated who you are and what makes your business unique and compelling; you have identified your ideal customers and what it is they need from you; and you have isolated the best tone and language to communicate to them that you can take away their pain. It's only after we've laid that necessary groundwork that we can explore the fourth pillar of the Marketing RAMP: the relationship stages that occur as customers go on their journey (see Figure 7.1).

Figure 7.1. The fourth pillar of the Marketing RAMP.

Working on this fourth pillar of the RAMP helps you follow and keep track of the natural, dynamic progression of marketing rather than succumb to the path of least resistance, sending out masses of unwanted and trite communications in the form of emails, text messages, and possibly even direct mail. This work will help you pivot and refine your approach with each piece of real-time feedback or information a prospect reveals. The goal is to turn new leads into lifelong fans of your brand.

In this chapter, I talk about the stages of this journey and the big picture of how Pillar 4 fits into a Marketing RAMP. In Parts II and III, I dive into the details of each stage.

TEN STAGES OF THE RELATIONSHIP JOURNEY

The relationship between a business and a customer evolves over ten specific, defined stages, each calling for its own cadence, communication style, and strategy. Here's a brief description of each stage (see also Figure 7.2):

1. First impression: This is how new leads enter into a relationship with your brand. It's their first point of contact, and you better make sure it's good.

2. Pain point segmentation: Here, we must get to know our customers and understand what it is that motivates them, so we can act with intention and strategy. Otherwise, we fall back into the trap of blindly talking at them rather than with them.

3. Tribal alignment: Build an alignment of values with the buyer by directly linking to their primary pain point. Doing so elicits their emotional investment, and a true bond starts to form.

4. Rapport: Create trust and attack the reptilian brain's internal objections. The goal here is to cement the consumer into our brand's tribe.

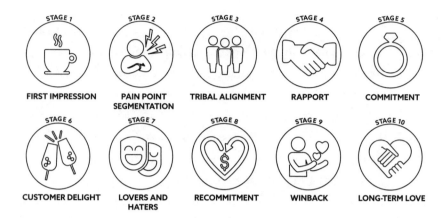

Figure 7.2. The ten stages of Pillar 4 of the Marketing RAMP.

5. Commitment: We hope that our relationship with our ideal customer is strong enough, and we present our proposal, asking the prospect to commit to us and purchase what it is we're offering. This stage captures our plan for what happens when the buyer says "yes" to our proposal.

6. Customer delight: It is your job to assure your new customer they've made the right choice and to battle the negative forces of self-doubt and buyer's remorse that spring up in over 60 percent of the people who purchase from you.[12] This is the honeymoon phase, where we remove buyer's remorse and create a delightful after-purchase sequence.

7. Lovers and haters: Honest feedback is invaluable, and we must be brave enough to ask for it. If we've modeled Stage 6 correctly, very few customers will be unhappy. Regardless, we need to be prepared for any answer and have a plan in place for how to respond.

---

12 See, for example, Richard Laycock and Catherine Choi, "Black Friday Statistics, 2022," *Finder*, November 7, 2022, https://www.finder.com/black-friday-statistics. *Slickdeals* says that buyer's remorse after online shopping can reach 74 percent. See Kevin Payne, "What Are Americans' Biggest Online Shopping Regrets?," *Slickdeals*, March 28, 2022, https://money.slickdeals.net/surveys/online-shopping-regrets-2022-survey/.

8. Recommitment: A customer committed to us once by making a purchase and hopefully telling us they're happy that they did. We have to assume they'll be willing to do so again. We're not looking for one-time customers; we're looking for a lifelong relationship. This stage is about getting a buyer to say "yes" all over again.

9. Winback: Sometimes, things go wrong, and prospects fall away from their customer journey. Whether it was your fault, theirs, or simply an issue of timing, we want to pursue those missed connections and former flames and reignite their intrigue with us. This stage represents a fork in the road and wakes us up at the right time to ideally reengage those who never bought and those who only bought once.

10. Long-term love: This stage represents what most marketers call long-term nurture. People are not plants; people desire love. Your work in this stage is to masterfully craft a way to nurture the relationship, which is tied to a content calendar, seasonal events, and your brand. You'll be drawing from a powerhouse of content to connect and convert every single month of the year.

There are two important features of the ten stages that I want to point out: the way that the stages mimic human relationships and the fact that you should not expect the journey to be linear.

Mimicking Human Relationships

I think of the first five stages of the relationship journey as the work necessary to get your customers to commit. The last five stages are how to ensure they stay committed. I've based the first five stages on science, mirroring the stages humans pass through as they fall in love and become committed to one another:

1. Initiation: Following a positive first impression, the attraction is sparked, and the romance begins.

2. Experimentation: Two parties cautiously get to know each other, assessing each other's words, actions, and body language.

3. Intensification: Guards start to come down as emotional investment begins to take place, and the seed of trust is planted.

4. Integration: There is a merging together as the other person is vetted and found to be in alignment with what you want.

5. Bonding: After doing one's due diligence, the time has come for a formal commitment.

Figure 7.3 shows the links between the formation of human relationships and the first five stages of the customer journey captured in the fourth pillar.

Along every point in the first five stages of the journey, you will need to prove that a relationship with your brand adds value to their life. Value exchange is a mandatory element for any relationship to survive. With an exchange of value, trust can then be established. If our ideal customers are receiving value from their relationship with us and beginning to trust that we can satisfy their needs, we have everything we need to ask for their commitment (the solution we've presented to them). The logic behind these first stages is to deliver value in some form to the customer, establish trust, show social proof, address the risks a prospect links to making a purchase, and then proceed with the "ask." You can always ask them to purchase along the entire communication process, but going in for the big "ask" right away is sure to turn off the majority of prospective customers who encounter your company.

Stages 6 to 10 are present because everybody knows that a relationship doesn't end at the moment of commitment. In fact, that's really just the beginning. You don't suddenly pull back your energy and your efforts, expecting your new partner to continue being faithful, present, and

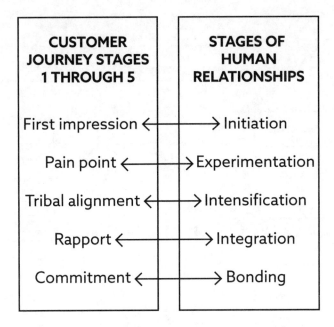

Figure 7.3. The five scientific stages of human relationships and how they connect to the first five stages of the customer journey.

supportive while your attention moves elsewhere. Healthy, lasting relationships require continued reassurance, investment, and prioritization.

The Journey Will Not Be Linear

Unlike a funnel, the relationship journey used as part of a RAMP acknowledges that customers rarely follow a linear progression and that each journey likely takes a different course. While Figure 7.2 depicts the ten stages as a straight series of steps, any given customer is unlikely to go through all ten or to proceed through them in order.

In part, this is because your marketing communications will not be perfect, and customers will not know at first if you are a good fit for them. So not every customer in Stage 1 will necessarily proceed into Stage 2, and so on.

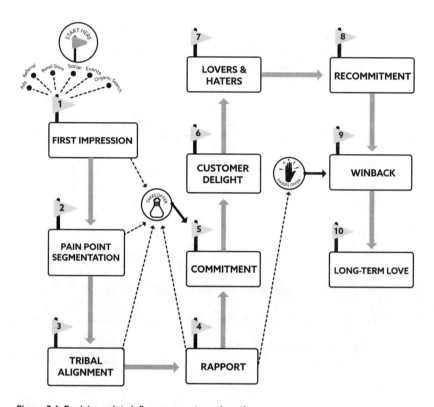

Figure 7.4. Decision points influence a customer's path.

Second, the map encompasses several decision points, as shown in Figure 7.4. Some customers may jump to commitment—accept your offer—sooner than others and skip one or more of the first five stages. Also, prospects can fall off the path at any point, so you'll have to jump ahead to recommitment or winback to see if you can get them back on board.

Having each stage of the process mapped out still carries great value, even if the customer doesn't move through them in order. Instead of needing to write and send hundreds of emails or texts, you can shape your CRM program to implement the decisions you've laid out in your Marketing RAMP. Most responses can be automatic, triggering the appropriate communications in a personalized fashion for each individual in their own unique stage within their journey. Once we take the time to know where a customer fits—where they're coming from and where in their journey they are—the RAMP determines when and how your CRM will automatically take over so customers will be guided where they need to go next, according to their own desires. Time is not spent rewriting duplicate emails, sending endless texts, or leaving repetitive voicemail messages. Balls are never dropped.

AVOIDING STAGNATION

The information you gather around your customers' journeys will help you define and adhere to the ideal maximum duration of your digital marketing efforts. Because the goal is to move away from the impersonalized and inconsiderate tunnel deluge, we must take note and adjust when a customer journey stagnates.

When we talk with the prospect about the same thing multiple times, and they are not clicking, not taking any action, or not giving us any kind of response, they are telling us that they're not interested. We need to know when to switch gears and start communicating more effectively with the prospect. If an email has gone unanswered for a week, for example, the prospect may have lost interest, be on vacation, or perhaps is occupied with a business or personal crisis. We need to ask them what's happening without making assumptions, but we also need to move this person to another stage of the journey before they disengage forever. Therefore, we must change the conversation.

When I ask prospective clients about the ideal and maximum duration of their marketing communications, I'm often met with blank faces. Many business owners are only familiar with sales funnels, and funnels can't engage responsively with prospects. They just keep pounding on the door until someone answers or unsubscribes.

Pillar 4 of the Marketing RAMP is designed to deal with this issue. Suppose you own an investment advisory company and have a prospect who has gone silent. The journey-based information built into your CRM should prompt you to send them another email asking if they have thought more about their investing criteria, inquiring if perhaps their goals have changed. This could receive the response: "Yes, that's it. I've decided I only want to invest in real estate." Now, we know how to communicate with our prospect, and we are back on the path to turning them into a client.

SELLING VERSUS OFFERING

Before moving on to Parts II and III, where I discuss the details of each stage of the relationship journey, I want to comment on the overall purpose of taking the time to define that journey and using it to shape your marketing efforts.

Generally speaking, the customer journey should be marked by communications that convey openness and familiarity. This is where, again, our three guiding principles inform and direct us. By remaining mindful of the way human brains process information and develop relationships, we can make sure we don't devolve into "selling" the prospect anything. Instead, we "offer" solutions to help achieve their desired goal at critical stages along the buyer's journey.

That might seem like semantics. But as I see it, "selling" the prospect something indicates that we are cramming our desires, our agenda, and our needs down the prospect's throat—much like the traditional funnel model—until they either give in and buy or tell us to get lost. That's an ugly, primitive, and, perhaps most importantly, ineffective way to do business.

Instead, the goal is to earn their trust by explaining exactly how our product or service will solve their problems. With integrity, finesse, and skill, outstanding salespeople can match what their company offers to what their customer needs. They know how to dynamically engage with their prospects and customers in a manner that both educates and motivates them. That doesn't mean we don't employ persuasion. It simply means that you are keeping your customer's experience at the forefront when designing any communication.

When speaking with someone face to face, you can naturally pick up on signs that they may not be interested in a topic. When that happens, you change the subject to ensure that the conversation continues and both people enjoy the experience. This is basic human nature and exactly what the Marketing RAMP has been built to mimic.

A simple scenario that makes clear the difference between blindly selling and thoughtfully offering is eating at a restaurant. When you go out to eat, you want a good dining experience. If that's what you get—the ambience was great, the staff kind and attentive, the food tasty, and the service prompt—you will happily pay your bill at the end of the night. You wanted and received a great dining experience. The restaurant's agenda was identical to yours in providing a good dining experience. But by satisfying your needs, it was pursuing secondary goals: maximizing your bill and increasing the likelihood that you would dine at the restaurant in the future. Yet, you didn't feel "sold to" at all. You enjoyed yourself and ate a great meal. You felt that you received value and that your money was well spent.

Now, consider the opposite. You go out to eat at that same restaurant, but now with rude staff and long wait times. Despite you clearly being unhappy, they aggressively try to upsell you throughout the night—appetizers, specials of the day, specialty cocktails, desserts, food to take home to your dog, after-dinner drinks—regardless of what you say to them. Like a sales funnel, they hammer you with robotic talk and are completely indifferent to what you want at the moment. It doesn't matter how delicious the food is. At the end of the night, you bitterly pay your bill and walk out knowing you'll never be back. You might even be so frustrated as to leave a negative online review.

Experience is everything.

In today's modern digital world, businesses cannot hide. Sooner rather than later, your customers will tell you exactly how they feel about you. They'll always do it with their wallets and, sometimes, with their voices, too. Both wield incredible power that can feed your business life or curse it into a dire existence. Doing the foundational work with the first three pillars of the RAMP (and using that information to help you shape what your business does as customers build relationships with you) will increase your chances of success.

CREATING A SAFE SPACE ALONG THE JOURNEY

Remember my Volkswagen Bug? After I understood how the engine and all the parts worked, I was able to get it running! And through that process I gained knowledge that has paid dividends still to this day. Engines can get more complicated, but at their core, they all function the same way. They must intake fuel and then convert that fuel into power. The result of that power creates energy and motion.

The concept of the customer journey isn't simply a general guiding framework. Whether or not you curate the journey—actively guide customers through the process—it exists. Optimizing this journey for both your customer and yourself as you build a relationship holds the key to your company's success, likely even its survival.

When it comes to defining the customer journey, we need to remember that while we're committed to treating customers with integrity and respect, many other companies aren't doing the same. This means that we will likely encounter consumers who have been battered and bruised by companies who endlessly took from them without providing value in return. Understandably, this might have left them on the defensive. They may fear that if they give you an inch, you'll aggressively claim a mile.

Ideally, as your customers travel on their journey with your business, your brand can become interwoven into the fabric of their lives. Think about some of the most iconic brands of the past hundred years. "Kleenex" was genericized to mean any paper handkerchief. "Escalator" became synonymous with a moving walkway. "Thermos" now refers to any vacuum flask. When we ask someone to look something up on the internet, we say, "Google it." When I need to get to the airport from my hotel, I "Uber" there.

Top-tier brands often have at least one thing in common: we associate their name with a generic action or product. On a smaller scale, local brands can be just as powerful as these worldwide giants. The challenge for all of us is how we build the foundation of a brand (one email, phone call, text message, or video at a time) that will leave a lasting legacy of the work we've done.

To reiterate a point made earlier, the customer journey portion of the Marketing RAMP absolutely relies on having a CRM system in place for the best possible results. A CRM with marketing capabilities collects demographic and other pertinent information about your prospects and customers and then allows you to schedule emails, texts, and phone messages with them. Consider the CRM the vault in which you store your most precious assets—everything you need to know to make your customers and future customers happy, make them buy from you, and make them share your business with everyone they know. Without it, you're storing your most precious assets in the open, allowing them to be lost, or worse, taken from you by your competitors.[13]

 ## TOP TAKEAWAYS

1. The Marketing RAMP's customer journey has ten distinct, formulaic stages, each with its own timeline, communication style, and strategy.

2. Unlike traditional marketing techniques that often leave consumers feeling weary and battered, the RAMP's customer journey dynamically responds and adjusts according to prospect actions, cultivating an environment of integrity and respect.

3. There is a difference between selling versus offering value. Selling without truly offering value not only is outdated but also fails to create a bond with buyers. Your business must employ value

---

13 If you want to make sure you've got the right vault in place for your business, we've got some opinions on the ones we like to use. Check them out at www.marketingramp.com/crm.

creation before, during, and after a sale to ensure that you are establishing bonds with your buyers. The Marketing RAMP's stages ensure you do this every time.

4. People don't move through each of the ten stages in a calm and orderly manner—but you don't have to worry about monitoring that, because the RAMP does it for you when built using a CRM.

5. Having a CRM (customer relationship management) system in your business to collect and store prospective customer, past customer, and current customer data is critical to your business success and also powers the Marketing RAMP.

PART II

Getting a Commitment from the Customer

IMAGINE SOMEONE YOU DIDN'T KNOW WALKED up to you and said, "I know I just met you, but let's get married." They'd be seen as juvenile at best and more than a bit crazy at worst. Yet, in the marketing world, that's exactly what's happening. A lead or prospect makes the slightest hint of interest and is bombarded by "Buy now!" messages.

We've forgotten who is actually receiving our communications—real people. And real people don't just run out and choose a random stranger to get married to. So why in the world would we be so irrational with our marketing approach? We skip the wooing stage of a relationship and go for gold, requesting commitment entirely too early. No wonder potential customers too often run for the hills.

Even if a company creates great products and puts out wonderful ads that engage its intended audiences, it will fail to achieve even a fraction of its potential without putting in the necessary groundwork for relationship building. That's what the first five stages of Pillar 4 are all about: shifting a prospect from not being in a relationship with you at all to making a commitment.

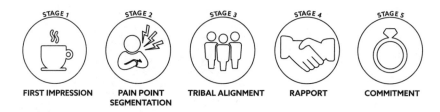

STAGE 1	STAGE 2	STAGE 3	STAGE 4	STAGE 5
FIRST IMPRESSION	PAIN POINT SEGMENTATION	TRIBAL ALIGNMENT	RAPPORT	COMMITMENT

Figure II.1. The first five stages of the relationship journey.

In everyday life, the power of connection in conversation is found in micro-moments. Unfortunately, too often, that magic is lost when the conversation takes place between a brand and a person. While we may never be able to fully recreate within a marketing campaign the magic between two humans, we can absolutely mimic the most important elements. That's why, from the get-go, the Marketing RAMP framework guides you in how to take the emotional response of your prospects into consideration—to help you get past the reptilian brain. This is just one of many major differences you'll see between the outdated traditional marketing approach and this revolutionary new approach.

This part of the book begins with a chapter on prework that you'll find helpful in allowing you to establish an emotional connection with your prospects. The remaining five chapters walk through the first five stages of the relationship journey, from first impressions to a commitment, as shown in Figure II.1.

TIP: ARE YOU TREATING YOUR CUSTOMERS RIGHT?

As you travel with a potential buyer during these first stages of the relationship-building journey, the overriding goal should be to create healthy, safe spaces for consumers at every stage along the way. If a prospect doesn't respond to your marketing messages or isn't answering questions, step back and consider if you're treating them right. Ask hard questions like the following:

- Are we providing true value?

- Are we addressing their fears and offering solutions?

- Are we infusing points of delight into the process that show we care about their well-being and we're not only here for the sale?

- If the answer to any of these questions is no, what needs to change?

Businesses must cut through the accumulated marketing baggage and create special moments for their customers that leave them saying, "This company is different. I like them. They're my people." A healthy digital relationship resembles a healthy real-world relationship more than most people realize.

CHAPTER 8

Prework for the Relationship Journey

IMAGINE I PRINTED OUT THE EMAILS you've been sending to your prospective and current customers. Then, I put you in a room with one of them, where you can speak using *only* the lines contained in those communications. Would you be embarrassed? Would they be confused? Is it maybe even off-putting? Would they think you were pushy and conceited, unable to make a real connection with another human being? Chances are, your answer is yes to at least one of these questions. When it comes to marketing, it's easy to forget that we're a human communicating to another human. It doesn't matter if you're sending your message through the internet, by direct mail, or by SMS. We want our communications to feel natural, warm, and welcoming.

That idea of connecting marketing to human experiences is the philosophy behind the Marketing RAMP system (see Figure 8.1). You want your business and customer communications to feel like you and the prospect are sitting down to have dinner or meeting up at a coffee shop for a casual conversation. (In other words, you're both going to enjoy it a lot more than whatever you're doing now.)

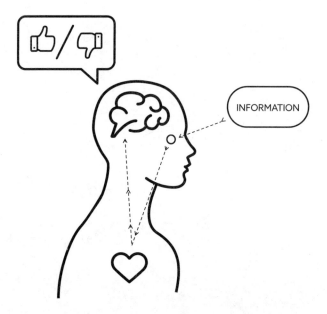

Figure 8.1. Information that creates strong emotions in the brain will elicit action.

It's tricky to make these human connections during the relationship-building process represented by the first five stages of the journey. I talk about the specifics of what to do in each stage in later chapters in Part II. But before going there, I want to encourage you to do some prework that will help you develop more effective communication pieces throughout the relationship journey. You can find the following prework elements in this chapter and Exercise 5:

1. Defining a Great Travesty that will immediately resonate with your ideal customer

2. Developing success stories that allow prospects to believe that *your* offerings are the solution to the pain points

3. Making sure you're clear about what you will ask the prospect to do (the call to action, or CTA) at each step along the way

DEFINING A GREAT TRAVESTY

A Great Travesty is a wrong that must be set right—an unjust situation, a threat, or an enemy that represents an ideal customer's ultimate frustration or challenge.

In the world of marketing, the Great Travesty is that too many marketing efforts do the exact opposite of what they are intended to do. Force-fed, packaged marketing messages make customers feel unheard, unappreciated, and unwilling to consider doing business with you.

Here's another example. Say the solopreneur of a small gardening business has been troubled by how most fertilizer and plant foods available contain chemicals toxic to humans, animals, and the environment. Over the years, he created an equally effective, nontoxic alternative. He used this personally at first and then began distributing locally as demand among his friends and neighbors grew. Then, finally, it went online. While the new nontoxic fertilizer was having some success, its price was double the cost of other premium plant food brands and quadruple the cost of the cheapest options on the market. And it came in significantly smaller quantities, to boot. The challenge: getting consumers to see why the higher price was worth paying.

It was immediately clear that the key to turning this company's marketing around was going to be its Great Travesty, which had to be centered around how the world we now live in is laced with chemicals. Gardeners, by and large, care about the environment. So this business needed to emphasize that the current solutions used in the marketplace contain chemicals that cause cancer and create birth defects, poisoning not only our own bodies but also our pets and our planet as a whole.

Many people who grow their own fruits and vegetables are this company's ideal customers, and they are motivated by a desire to know where their food comes from. These customers care that what they're using to grow food is organic and safe for themselves and the environment. These ideal customers would therefore connect to the Great Travesty and be open to hearing the company's solution, which was getting back to gardening that was healthier both in terms of what we eat and for the whole planet.

By winning over their reptilian brain, we're now able to communicate that this brand of fertilizer lasts longer and expands to four times the size of the bag's exterior once water has been added. Ultimately, it isn't as expensive as it seems. Only once customers have been aligned are they receptive to hearing about why it's the best option.

If you're reading this and wondering to yourself, "Can the Great Travesty be used in my business?" the answer is yes. Recently, I had a consultation with a prospective client who owns a marketing agency exclusively serving florists across the United States. His business had been doing incredible work for hundreds of independent florists. However, after COVID-19, and with the growing market domination of the big corporations advertising on TV, the small floral shops he serves were getting squeezed.

I talked with this business owner about how he needed to know his ideal customers' pain points and connect with them by articulating a Great Travesty. He was hesitant. He wasn't sure this approach would work and feared that having a bit of a negative slant would further push away his prospects who were already in a painful state. It took some convincing, but as we built his Marketing RAMP for him, he realized the Great Travesty was that the big corporations with national brand recognition had taken over the floral business. No longer do consumers call their local florist for flowers; they call 1-800 numbers or visit national, big-brand websites to order those flowers. These big brands are stealing the profits from the local florists, and worse, they then hire those florists to fulfill those orders with a drastically small profit margin. Not only is that hurting the mom-and-pop independent businesses, but it's impossible for them to fight off the big national brands with their multimillion-dollar marketing budgets.

This marketer was facing what seemed like an impossible, modern-day David-versus-Goliath battle. My company had to convince him and his small-business florists that it could be won, and it wouldn't cost them a fortune to do so. My client had the solution they needed to beat the big-name "order gatherers" at their own game. The independent florists could win back their own customers, thus enabling them to make more money and stay in business.

The results? By homing in on his prospects' pain points and then divulging the secret sauce to solve the problems captured in the Great Travesty—accompanied by success stories—the attendance of his online webinars skyrocketed, and his sales tripled within a week. His company had more work than it ever had. With that event and the post-event sales consultations, his business ballooned to numbers he had never seen before with a show rate that was 50 percent higher than his average.

Exercise 5 will help you define the Great Travesty for your business. Fortunately, you don't have to start from scratch—it can be informed by the work you already completed earlier in the RAMP. Following a simple formula, you must do the following:

- Remember that you're speaking to your ideal customer(s), identified earlier in the RAMP (see Chapter 3).

- Explain a typical experience they've likely encountered that they will immediately recognize.

- Highlight the Great Travesty, explain how it's wrong, and indicate its need to be solved. (Tip: Revisit your Great Travesty descriptions as you learn more about your prospects and their pain points during the relationship journey.)

- State how you are solving this Great Travesty, drawing from your brand pitch and brand narrative work.

- Finish with a definitive statement on how your solution best rights their wrongs.

Your company's mission statement and value propositions must be in line with what you communicate here. If they aren't, your Great Travesty will fall flat, or perhaps even do damage. It is fundamental to the Great Travesty's efficacy that it connects to why you are doing what you are doing, whether that be why your company was founded or the purpose of the products or services you're providing.

CREATING POWERFUL SUCCESS STORIES

As I talk about in Chapter 1, the human brain is a fascinating work of art as it sorts through billions of bits of information, determining what makes it past the oldest part of our brain (what I labeled the gatekeeper) and what doesn't. The core of the brain is determined to avoid pain and the risk of potential pain at nearly all costs.

The civilization of mankind has been built on this guiding force, and that's why modern brands must understand what pains their ideal customer and then provide the solution that can directly solve that pain. Without doing so, the chance of the human brain making the decision to take a risk in purchasing a product or service is exponentially lower than a competitor's product that speaks directly to the reduction or aversion of pain.

Human beings are hardwired to relate to the world around them by chunking bits of information together, leaving only the relevant parts and discarding the rest. Chunking bits of information for the brain are optimized and craved for in the form of *storytelling*. If you've ever heard of memory champions or people who have incredible abilities to remember things, they always tell you that the way they can remember impossible amounts of numbers and details is by creating simple, relatable stories to cement the details into memory.

The power of storytelling is why testimonials are great, but success stories are even better. Think of testimonials as ultrashort stories that both educate and entertain your prospects and quickly get to the CTA ("We did _____, and our life is now great! You need to do the same today!"). But more detailed success stories are effective for two reasons.

First, people are hardwired to be drawn in by stories and to retain them. That's why, if I were to tell you a two-minute story, you could easily summarize it back to me. But if I tell you my phone number out loud, you will almost surely forget it immediately. With marketing, the story format works well, no matter what kind of business you're in or where in the world you are.

Second, from a psychological standpoint, going on and on about how great I am as I try to convince a prospect to do business with me is going to undo the work already done to break through the barrier of their reptilian mind. No one wants to be sold to like that, and their defenses will inevitably rise once again. But with success stories, it's not me talking at all. It's someone else, someone "just like you."

In short, our brains not only require but crave stories, and that is why you can remember something insignificant, like what mode of transport you used and where you stopped along the way to your last vacation, but you can't remember your best friend's phone number. Without the story in place to relate to the information, your brain will discard it.

I encourage you to look at your own communications from a customer's perspective. Is your company's messaging aligned with your customers' aspirational objectives and pain points? Do you also tell a great story? Most businesses don't. Identifying and cultivating a powerful brand voice will help your customers bond to your products or services both emotionally and rationally, and you'll make more sales doing so.

That is part of why your brand voice must be captured in the *social proof* that you offer your customers. Customers today are hungry for testimonials. I have a vested interest in them buying from me, so they don't want to hear *me* explain why my services are so great. Hearing only from the seller creates an imbalance where customers perceive their risk as greater than their reward if they act. Before they take further action, they will seek ways to eliminate as much risk as possible. One of the fastest methods for risk reduction is witnessing someone else—someone who has a relatable situation in life surrounding their pain point—take the risk first and assess the outcome. They'll want to hear about how John and Barbara used my services, how much better it made their lives, and why they recommend me. Suddenly, the reptilian brain relaxes. Other people who are similar to them let me in, and they survived—even thrived—because of it. The perceived risk is lower, and the reward seems promising.

In the Marketing RAMP, I call these testimonials *success stories* to emphasize that the most effective ones have a narrative arc. It's not just about smiling faces and an upbeat attitude. We want to communicate four pieces of information:

1. A customer had a pain.

2. They trusted us to help address it.

3. This is how we got rid of the pain.

4. They left feeling satisfied.

That simple formula is wildly effective in addressing the reptilian brain and can be employed on websites, in emails, in PDFs, and, best of all, in videos where happy clients tell your story for you.

A few years back, Built by Love worked with a leading sports medicine company on the East Coast. Its founder has worked with professional and Olympic athletes, celebrities, and many others. Prior to working with us, the company's website was poorly designed, and they had not worked out a simple way to explain what they did and how customers could benefit. Two of the most important aspects of our work with this company were (a) defining the Great Travesty (in this case, how injuries or chronic pain rob you of the freedom to do what you love), and (b) developing success stories that would connect with prospects and explain in a simple way what the company does.

The company now has a cache of first-person video success stories, told by the customers and by the company's experts. For each story, they developed a short-form video (approximately one minute) that hits the highlights and is designed to make an immediate emotional connection with viewers, as well as longer versions (three or more minutes) that go into more detail about the client's situation and how the company helped. For example, one of their clients was a woman who developed chronic back pain following a car accident. The two videos featuring this customer follow the four-part success story format I've outlined:

1. *A customer had a pain (quite literally in this case):* The woman describes what she's been through because of the car accident and the chronic pain issues she developed as a result. This is a brief statement in the short video (enough to make an emotional connection). She goes into more detail in the long version, detailing the kinds of issues that others in pain will understand.

2. *They trusted the company to help address it:* In the short video, the woman simply says that the sports medicine company helped eliminate her pain. In the longer version, she explains that she saw several physicians and physical therapists without success (customer frustration!) until a friend recommended this sports medicine company.

3. *How the company got rid of the pain:* This element is skipped in the short video. In the longer version, the company's expert explains how they took a full history of the woman's issues and used alternative medicine practices to address neural issues, not just muscular or skeletal issues. The woman comments that the company stood out because they looked at not only her injury but also her lifestyle and gave her a path to get back to "what I love to do."

4. *The customer left feeling satisfied:* The woman talks about her lifestyle now that she is pain-free, including her ability to be an active mom to three young children, and we learn that she has even become a spin instructor. She very clearly endorses the company ("If you want to achieve the next level, [this company] is the place to be").

The message comes across clearly: people who are frustrated because they can no longer do what they enjoy doing because of pain or injury can regain those passions by working with this company. What more could you ask of a customer testimonial?

IDENTIFY YOUR CALLS TO ACTION

Many businesses underestimate the importance of CTAs. They assume people are up to the task of making simple connections and reaching out when they're ready. However, this is a grave misstep. As humans living in a digital era, we are overwhelmed with constant content and communications, and we are almost always multitasking. As a result, our attention is yanked in every direction. What seems straightforward to you (the business owner or marketer) likely is not obvious to the busy, distracted prospect. It's better to spell out, as simply as possible, exactly what you want them to do and when they should do it.

One important tip here: *Keep the CTA options simple.* Here's why.

One afternoon, inside an upscale food market, shoppers were offered free samples of gourmet jam. Little did they know that they were participating in one of the most famous research studies (by psychologists Sheena Iyengar and Mark Lepper) on the paradox of choices. What they found is that more options are not always better. In fact, presenting fewer options to the shoppers not only maintained the same number of samples tried but, surprisingly, increased the sale of the gourmet jams by tenfold.[14]

The findings of this research are nothing short of magical for marketers. It is crucial to understand that making many options available to your customers will likely lead to them feeling anxiety surrounding making the wrong decision and then regretting it. That's why it's our job to understand what our customers need and why and then guide them simply and smoothly to the decision that's right for them.

14 Sheena S. Iyengar and Mark R. Lepper, "When Choice Is Demotivating: Can One Desire Too Much of a Good Thing?," *Journal of Personality and Social Psychology* 79, no. 6 (2009): 995–1006.

In the unlikely case that there was any confusion on this front, anxiety is the last emotional response we want to trigger in our prospects. Avoiding this stress response is accomplished by correctly identifying your customers' pain points and resisting the urge to overcomplicate the path forward for prospects at every step along their journey.

In short, giving people too many options makes them second-guess themselves. It overwhelms them, and their reptilian brain shuts it down after deciding that sifting through the information isn't worth it. Their internal objections (the ongoing self-conversation in their mind debating whether they're going to do something or not) win out. They don't engage with us. And, ultimately, they don't buy.

That's why in every communication with your prospects, you will want to be clear about what it is you expect of them—what the call to action (CTA) is.

 TOP TAKEAWAYS

1. The relationship journey defined in the RAMP relies on your ability to make meaningful connections with your ideal customers through your communications.

2. The fodder for those communications comes from the following prework:

   a. Defining a Great Travesty that succinctly captures the "wrong that must be set right" relating to the prospect's business goals

   b. Creating powerful success stories that describe a customer's pain point, why the customer trusted your business, how you got rid of the pain, and how the customer felt afterward

   c. Identifying a limited number of CTAs that you emphasize in your emails and other communications

EXERCISE 5: DEFINING A GREAT TRAVESTY AND BUILDING POWERFUL SUCCESS STORIES

The Great Travesty and success stories are elements you will need to refer to repeatedly throughout the relationship journey. You can refine and add to them as you work through the RAMP, but it's helpful to take a first pass before you do the rest of the work.

Define a Great Travesty

- Review the descriptions of your ideal customers. (This should already be documented in your Marketing RAMP.)

- Explain a typical frustrating experience they've encountered that they will immediately recognize or an ongoing challenge they seem unable to overcome. (This can be found in the "their relationship to you" section.)

- Call out the Great Travesty from the previous statement and state how it's wrong and needs to be solved.

Develop Powerful Success Stories

1. Find an ideal customer who suffered challenges typical of other ideal customers.

2. Have them share about trying other fixes in the past that did not work and how hopeless they felt, as if nothing was going to resolve their issue. Here is a recommended sequence of questions to ask:

   - Tell me about the time before you came to us.

   - What did you need that you didn't have?

   - How did that make you feel?

   - What was it like when you finally discovered the solution?

   - The process to get here was great, right?

   - What was the end result?

- How do you feel about it compared to where you started?

- What would you tell someone who is struggling like you used to?

TIP: CAPTURE CUSTOMERS ON VIDEO TELLING THEIR SUCCESS STORIES

As the videos I describe in the previous chapter illustrate, it is wildly effective to capture success stories in video form. You can even send a template based on this formula to your customers to insert their testimonial statements into the blank spaces. With very little effort, you now have an incredibly powerful video testimonial to work with. (That said, anything that comes to you as a video can easily be turned into a written success story and vice versa.) Watching this type of content, a prospect is going to be blown away, thinking, "Wow, their story is just like mine, and look how well they're doing now. Man, I need to call this guy and do that thing!"

Document Their Story Using the Narrative Arc

- *Meet the ordinary hero:* Introduce the hero with a short background story (one to two sentences).

- *Tribal alignment:* Create an alignment of the hero with the reader (one to two sentences).

- *Learn the backstory:* Tell what their life was like before they acted. Their life needs to be filled with uncertainty, pain, frustration, and may also include lost time, money, or opportunities (two to three sentences).

- *The hero falls:* The hero finally hit a breaking point in which they needed to act and change their painful state (one to two sentences).

- *The hero hesitates:* They had tried to fix their painful state before and been burned, so they were reluctant to try and fail again (one to two sentences).

- *The epiphany:* Then they discovered [your company or product name], and this felt different because of [reason why it was different or your company's secret sauce] (two to three sentences).

- *The hero acts:* They acted and purchased your product or service and immediately they noticed this was indeed different. Their experience felt better, and their internal objections from the Brand Voice section melted away (two to three sentences).

- *Ordinary hero transforms into an extraordinary hero:* Now life is great, and their pain is removed. They now live the [aspirational outcome] that any ideal customer in this [category of interest] desires (two to three sentences).

- *Hero calls you to action:* A quote from the hero that directly calls out your ideal customers, addressing their reluctance to act and confirming that things are much better once they buy or take action with [your company or product] (one sentence).

- *Closing the loop:* A direct, aspirational call to action now drives the reader into action to be like the hero and follow the specific CTA (one sentence). The last statement the customer makes in this story should be that if anyone is reading or listening to their story and are in a similar situation, their advice is to "Act now. You'll be thankful you did!"

Once you package the answers to these questions, you have real people telling real people: "We're so happy. You can be too if you do this. Why wait?" We talk more about the staggering power of the success story once we get to the rapport stage (Chapter 12).

CHAPTER 9

Stage 1: First Impression

You've got one chance to make a first
impression that lasts a lifetime.

I WAS MEETING WITH A FINANCIAL advisor for the first time when he said, "Mr. Bussius, how much money do you wish to have when you retire?" I looked at him wide-eyed and overwhelmed. I was ready and motivated to save, but I had no idea how to answer that question.

Leaving his office forty-five minutes later, I reflected on why I had such a negative impression of this advisor and why our meeting had felt so unproductive and frustrating. I realized that while saving for retirement was very much on my mind, I'm someone who places a high value on experiences. When I envision my retirement years, I see myself traveling, spending quality time with my family, and enjoying my favorite hobbies. I don't think of it in terms of a dollar amount sitting in some bank account somewhere.

Rather than connecting with me in a way that represented a Great Travesty or a pain point, the financial advisor simply repeated the same question over and over.

The outcome would have been quite different if he had said, "There are a lot of people like you who aren't sure how or how much to save for retirement. It can be scary. I'm here to help and make sure your investment will create the kind of lifestyle you want to have in retirement." He could have then said, "Before we talk about money, tell me how you'd like to spend your retirement years. What activities do you want to enjoy? Do you want to travel? In what fashion and frequency?" That would have engaged me and given me the impression that this was an advisor who really cared about me as an individual. I would have felt he was equipped to help address my pain points. I then would have responded, and our dialogue would have progressed into a very productive arena where he and I could then put numbers to my aspirations of a retirement lifestyle. If we did that, there's no question he would have secured my business. Instead, he left me feeling more anxious about the very thing I had hoped he'd help with. And guess what I did? Nothing. I was overwhelmed, frustrated, and wasn't sure what to do. So I did what all people do when they're overwhelmed; I stayed in my current state and took no action for change.

There's an old saying often attributed to Will Rogers that goes, "You never get a second chance to make a good first impression." I couldn't agree with him more. This premise should, therefore, inspire a masterfully engineered experience within every business's marketing efforts. When a prospective customer encounters your brand for the very first time, you've got one chance to create an impression that is better than your competition can deliver. If a customer's experience with another brand is better, they'll have little reason to pay further attention to you, let alone actually give you their business.

That's why Stage 1 of the customer journey is all about making a positive first impression (see Figure 9.1). This chapter and Exercise 6 help you identify what you want for your own first impression.

EVERY JOURNEY BEGINS WITH A FIRST IMPRESSION

Cultivating a stellar customer experience begins the moment a new lead enters your company's world, no matter how they got there, either digitally or physically. Most businesses have more than one route in place

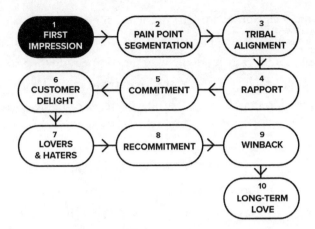

Figure 9.1. Stage 1 of the ten stages in the relationship journey: first impression.

for this to happen. But in this day and age, the majority of new leads are generated through digital means, such as the following:

- Organic web browsing

- Paid advertising

- Referrals

- Special event or promotions

- Social media

- Walk-ins (for brick-and-mortar businesses)

But with all these avenues, the first impression you offer should be designed to get the prospect to opt in (i.e., execute a CTA), thank them if they do, and offer them something of value in exchange for providing their contact information or connecting to your CRM.

The Thank-You

When a customer executes the CTA, show appreciation. Maybe you send them a handwritten thank-you card. They might see a GIF showing an explosion of confetti in the order confirmation along with a link to a video that thanks customers for entrusting in the company's brand. You could even send them some company-branded gear in a specially designed box along with a handwritten card inside, as my agency does for new clients. The key here is bringing a delightful surprise to the experience to once again show that you are different and value your customers.

Imagine filling out an online form, and instead of the standard thank-you screen that you so often see, a short video begins to play. "Hey, this is the founder. I'm so excited you've scheduled a consult. Whether we work together or not, I'm looking forward to having a conversation with you." With minimal effort, you have just entirely transformed the way your company's first impression is recorded in that person's mind.

Videos are one of my favorite mediums, because you can communicate so much more with your tonality, your voice, and your facial expressions than you can through text alone. You can also build a relationship with your viewers through video. Have you ever seen screaming fans waiting outside for hours to get a glimpse of a celebrity? I have, and I'm sure you have, too. Have you ever wondered why so many people are so emotional over celebrities whom they've never spoken to? The celebrity doesn't even know this person exists. Yet, the fan has formed such strong feelings and opinions about them. It's because they have formed a relationship by seeing them in video. They feel that they know this person, and it's the power of video that can do this so effectively. Studies show that more than 70 percent of communication is nonverbal. A famous research study conducted by a UCLA psychology professor emeritus named Albert Mehrabian found that 7 percent of communication relies on the words being said, 30 percent depends on vocal elements and intonation, and 55 percent relies on facial cues.[15]

---

15 Albert Mehrabian, *Silent Messages: Implicit Communication of Emotions and Attitudes*, 2nd ed. (Belmont, CA: Wadsworth, 1980).

What does this mean for you and your marketing? If you really want to ensure that your message is going to have the best possible chances of getting across to your ideal customers and you want to form strong relationships with them, you better be thinking about videos in your arsenal of communications and within your marketing mix.

Something of Value

Besides offering a heartfelt thank-you, you want to offer the new lead something of value, which should be a lead magnet. This can take different forms, depending on your business:

- A PDF with useful proprietary information or insights the customer may not be able to get easily from another source

- A complimentary course

- Exclusive video or audio content

- A discount code to apply to a purchase

- An unbiased review of your product or service from a trusted source (such as a *Consumer Reports* article on an SUV you're selling)

Warning: If the "something of value" is *not* perceived that way by your prospect, then you've blown your first impression. If the prospect responds to your message and does gain value from the "something," this immediately opens the door for you to meaningfully engage with them. You can follow up to check, "Did you get it? Did you like it? Was it helpful? Do you have questions or comments?" This is also an opportunity to use some of the copy generated from the earlier pillars of the Marketing RAMP, such as the "We Serve" and "Who Need" statements from the brand pitch. An email response focused on those themes is simple and straightforward.

WHAT IT LOOKS LIKE TO GET STAGE 1 RIGHT

All lead magnets should contain some version of your brand pitch (Exercise 4) and also have a call to action (CTA) making clear what it is you want the prospect to do next—whether that's reserving a table to dine, booking a free consultation, or shopping at an online store. People are overwhelmed and busy juggling the many inputs of daily life. It's a mistake to assume they'll figure out and take that next step on their own. We want to remove as many barriers as possible and kindly guide them to the next stage of the journey.

Let's use an Italian restaurant as an example. When a prospective diner (new lead) connects with the restaurant's online system, they instantly receive a one-time coupon for 20 percent off their next meal (the something of value offered), along with a short video that introduces the prospect into the restaurant's culture and emphasizes the key features of what makes their establishment different from its competitors. The video tells the prospect, "We are not another soulless Italian chain restaurant. We serve authentic Sicilian cuisine from the Old Country. For three generations, our family has cooked with only the freshest, highest-quality ingredients for people with discerning tastes. There will be no bagged pasta or sauces from a jar here."

Two days later, the prospect receives an email describing the restaurant's to-go menu and service.

Another two days later, a third email informs the prospect about an intimate, exclusive lounge that has live jazz on the weekend and is adjacent to the main dining area.

So, within five days of entering their RAMP-based CRM, the prospect has been introduced to the wrong that must be righted—the Great Travesty, which, in this case, is the blight that is Americanized, mass-produced Italian food—and they have been given a gift and been educated on all the business-to-consumer products and services offered by the restaurant. The prospect has been shown that there is a better, more authentic alternative to the subpar chains they've been frequenting, and they're excited by that. They want to be considered someone of discerning taste.

There will also be people who come to you without opting in through one of your set lead magnets. Maybe they met you at a trade show or they emailed you directly because their friend told them about your business. Those people often get lost. Your RAMP must be designed to prevent that from happening. When a lead comes in through non-digital means, or outside the set online paths, the RAMP has a default Stage 1 (or lead magnet) sequence for that prospect.

For example, someone calls your business because they were referred to you by a friend. They did not opt in, and they are not in your database at all. Someone like this must be placed into the default Stage 1 response. This ensures that every single person who enters our world has a warm welcome and is delivered a gift of perceived value right in the beginning. First impressions are everything and the default Stage 1 delivers an experience that immediately sets us apart from our competition.

Typically, the default Stage 1 involves sending the prospect an email thanking them for their interest in the business and providing them one of the assets you already have on hand that you are confident is valuable to your ideal customers and also addresses a broad range of pain points that can be resolved when people buy or use your services. This welcoming sequence matters. First impressions are powerful, creating the foundation that the person's entire opinion of your brand will be built on.

Think of Stage 1 this way: When a welcomed guest arrives at your front door, what do you do? You warmly welcome them into your home and then you offer them a small gift, a gesture to show that they are welcome. That gift always goes something like this: "Can I get you something to drink? Are you hungry?" What you are actually doing is something very primal. Your actions and words show a guest that they are welcome; they are safe. You are offering them something for their own survival—food or water. This happens so naturally that we forget the power these simple courtesies have in addressing our need for survival.

Imagine if you knocked on the door of a friend and they didn't go through this common ritual. You certainly wouldn't feel very welcome, maybe even a bit alarmed. That's why we must treat all prospective customers with a warm welcome and a sign of appreciation. Stage 1 will ensure that no one in your business going forward feels anything but a warm welcome as their first impression.

EMBARKING ON THE JOURNEY

Remember that in a threatening situation, our human brain stops listening to what someone else is saying and rather exerts all its energy to mount a defense. This is because the reptilian brain must know it's safe and that there is something valuable to be had. Otherwise, it's going to focus its energies on fight or flight. In Stage 1, the primary goal is to get past that reptilian brain, speak words that buyers want to hear, and get them to understand that you are offering them something *they* will value. But this is not enough—yet.

What you are defining here is how you're going to make a good first impression and what your CRM will do to make sure that people move into Stage 2 if they do not take your first offer. All your existing Stage 1s should be viewed as micro-sequences that then flow directly into the Marketing RAMP's operating system, which is the foundational Stage 2. The only time this does not occur is when the prospects in Stage 1 do take the action or offer (typically a purchase or an appointment booking) presented to them. All others who fail to take that primary call to action should automatically be moved into Stage 2.

Your business should be creating many Stage 1 micro-sequences or pathways every year with a suggested new Stage 1 every month. The goal of all your Stage 1 actions is to entice a prospect to opt into communication with the company. Stage 1s that are developed with a pain point in mind can then be further segmented for marketing analysis to better understand which ones perform best. This will then dictate what future content and offers should be invested in and produced.

Though the odds are slim, it's possible that a first-impression contact will accept your call to action and go directly to the commitment

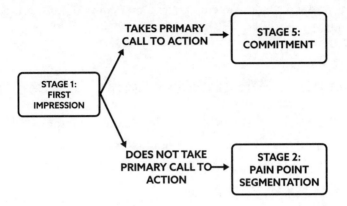

Figure 9.2. Stage 1: the process flow in your CRM.

stage. But most will not accept because we haven't really established a relationship with them, so your automated marketing system must dynamically move them into Stage 2 of the Marketing RAMP. The CRM flow is shown in Figure 9.2.

TOP TAKEAWAYS

1. You only get one chance to make a first impression on a prospect, and it's important to get it right.

2. From the moment someone embarks on their customer journey, you should be their protector and their guide, removing barriers from their path and telling them exactly where they're meant to go next.

EXERCISE 6: STAGE 1: FIRST IMPRESSION

Here are the exercises you'll want to take to develop your company's Stage 1 of the Marketing RAMP. This exercise is best done when you have completed the previous exercises, as each part of the RAMP builds on previous sections. It is not advised to skip steps because you'll miss critical components in content, strategy, and communication necessary for the highest rate of success.

Examine and Improve Your Current Stage 1 Inputs and Responses

- With a critical eye, inventory what you offer prospects (PDFs, helpful tips, free courses, discount offers, etc.). Are these perceived as value-added by the customer? If not, what changes do you need to make?

- Identify all forms of your lead generation, whether they be blog opt-ins, landing pages, webinars, web forms, contests, or something else.

- Classify each form of entry as a separate Stage 1 inside the Marketing RAMP and your CRM. (Stage 1 can and should have numerous versions.)

- Examine how you currently respond to a prospect. Are your responses unique to each Stage 1 entry pathway? Is the call to action clear? What improvements can you make?

TIP: EXAMINE THE SUCCESS OF PAST RESPONSES

- What data do you have on the success or failure of the kinds of responses you are offering now when a prospect enters your system? Which should you abandon?

- Do you have any data on how many or which types of prospects slip through the system (i.e., they do not receive an adequate response)?

Develop a Default Stage 1 Path

The default Stage 1 should be short and fast. You can achieve a great experience in as little as one email if your communication includes the following components:

- Thank them for their interest in the company.

- Communicate that you want to provide value to them regardless of whether they buy from you or not.

- Briefly mention the Great Travesty and show that you want to deliver on your mission of helping people like them with a valuable gift (the something of value).

- Offer them an opportunity to act on your primary call to action (what you really want them to do—buy something, book an appointment, etc.). Make sure to offer this in a nonaggressive, casual way. No one likes a pushy person they just met, and this includes your company.

CHAPTER 10

Stage 2: Pain Point Segmentation

Pain is the single most powerful driver for
human motivation that results in action.

I RECENTLY WITNESSED IN MY OWN family the perfect example of the
power of correctly—or in this case, incorrectly—identifying a pain point
and using it to connect with a prospect. After my son was born, my wife
began to worry that her compact sedan was not safe enough to transport
our baby. She decided that she wanted a roomier, sturdier SUV that was
highly rated for safety. And so it was that on a Saturday afternoon, we
headed to the dealership to look at a certain make and model she had
heard was renowned for its safety features.

My wife, an introvert, had asked me to do the talking. And when
the sales representative greeted us, I told him that she was looking for a
spacious SUV that would easily accommodate a car seat and was highly
rated for its safety features. I made it clear that the vehicle was going to
be driven exclusively by my wife, and that her main concern was safety. I
was just there to give a second opinion and watch over our son while she
test-drove the models she was interested in.

To me, a professional marketer, I had just handed this sales rep the easiest sale in the world. I made it abundantly clear who was buying the car and what pain point was driving (pun intended) her actions. And yet, he still managed to get it wrong.

When he walked us over to the SUVs, he immediately started pushing all the fancy options and upgrades available. He talked up the stereo features, the fancy features, including the heated leather seats, and the engine's horsepower. I watched my wife's face while he talked, and I could see her eyes glazing over. She could not have cared less about anything the sales rep was telling her, and so he started directing his stream of facts at me. But I wasn't even the one buying the car.

My wife was lukewarm through the whole process, and we ended up leaving the dealership without test-driving a single SUV. The man at the dealership was missing the mark on how to connect with his prospect. Without grasping and addressing the pain point driving the specific person he was dealing with, it wouldn't have mattered how great his sales pitch was. At that point, he had lost the sale.

However, I ended up rescuing the sale for the dealer. At home, I convinced my wife that she needed to go back and test-drive some vehicles. We returned later that day with my wife even less engaged. But toward the end of the test-drive, the salesperson casually mentioned, "There hasn't been a single death in this model to date because it's built to be so safe." That was it! My wife was sold. She drove off the lot with that car the same day.

If the salesperson had truly listened to our words when we first walked up, rather than adopting his one-size-fits-all sales approach, he could have mentioned that single fact hours earlier and clinched the sale in minutes. It's impossible to overstate the power of understanding a person's pain point and of being able to segment your prospects based on their different pain points so you can tailor your communications to their concerns.

However, connecting with a prospective buyer has to go beyond a simple understanding. Once you have identified and confirmed what

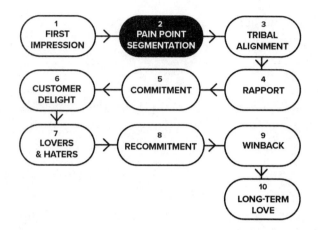

Figure 10.1. Stage 2 of the ten stages in the relationship journey: pain point segmentation.

your ideal customers' primary pain points are, it is your job to convince them that you share the same values they do and you're on the same side. You need them to see you as an ally, not a foe or competitor. That is the goal of pain point segmentation, which is Stage 2 of the relationship journey (see Figure 10.1).

At this point, if the prospect did not take the offer presented within the first stage—and the statistical probability is that they have not—the RAMP will make sure your CRM dynamically moves them automatically into the second stage: pain point segmentation. You knew how to speak their language well enough for them to accept your invitation to hop aboard your customer journey. Now, you need to prove to them that their choice to give you their time was a worthwhile decision. That's what Stage 2 and Exercise 7 are all about.

THE POWER OF PAIN

Why focus on pain points? Pain registers three times more powerfully in our memory than pleasure.[16] We don't want to use that manipulatively

---

16 David Gal and Derek Rucker, "The Loss of Loss Aversion: Will It Loom Larger than Its Gain?," *Journal of Consumer Psychology* 28, no. 3 (2018): 497–516.

or skew our content to trigger negative feelings in our prospects. But we need to keep the reptilian brain in mind and remember that what resonates with people—what gets them to take action—is the elimination and avoidance of pain. We must then categorize each new lead into one of our predetermined ideal customer groups so we can address the specific pain points associated with that subset of people.

From the pain point, we can start to make the connection between what the buyer is experiencing and the solutions we offer. We can assert that we're the expert, and we can put forward the offer that's most relevant to them. The Marketing RAMP is designed to inform the prospect what your business does and what's in it for them. We want to make that clear from the start. If we're not transparent, trust will not grow, the prospect is going to start questioning us, and they will adopt a skeptical demeanor.

If you need insight into what your customers' primary pain points are, it is absolutely okay to reach out and ask them. However, you want to do this in a way that makes clear how it benefits them to answer your question. Without doing this, you are introducing a friction point because you're asking them to do you a favor without having earned the right to ask for any favors. So we must pose the question in a way that makes clear why we want to know about their pain and how taking the time to answer is going to make their life easier. Here is an example message:

> For us to deliver best-in-class experiences and [products or services] that match your lifestyle and needs, please take a moment to let us know how we can best serve you. This will enable us to custom-tailor solutions you'll find value in. [Button leading to web form]

The web form that prospects get directed to if they respond to a Stage 2 communication must be direct, simple, and centered around the core pain points that you believe your business can solve. We are looking to gain critical insight into the main drivers pushing our prospects to us. Once we have that, we can custom-tailor our offering and our communication (including our success stories) to be focused on each prospect's specific pain point. This is precisely what we would be doing in real life, so why wouldn't our marketing system do the same thing?

TIP: ASK QUESTIONS!

A series of simple questions, paired with the promise of relief, can help avoid eliciting a stress response from your own prospects. While people desire instant gratification, they will settle for delayed gratification if the messaging says their lives will be better and pain will be avoided down the line if they first do this small action.

You can start a conversation or send an email saying, "Hey, for us to give you best-in-class services, we'd love to hear why you initially reached out and whether we're providing the solutions you were looking for." If you tell your customers that you're asking for their input to provide a more tailored solution, they're going to feel taken care of and motivated to share their insight with you. That said, it's okay if they don't respond. We can always assign them to the default track; we just want to give them an opportunity to share more first.

PAIN POINT SEGMENTATION

One of the most important facets of interaction that occurs when two people engage in conversation is each party listening to what the other person has to say and then crafting a response with the goal to create a valuable exchange of information. It's impossible to provide value in our conversations if we are not gauging what the other person's goals and desires are.

The goal of the pain point segmentation stage is to be as human as possible and drive home a truly valuable conversation with the recipient.

To this end, we are going to do what every human does when they engage with someone else; we are going to learn what they want and then customize our response to them.

Suppose you make the decision to get into the best shape of your life. Your main goal is to lose the extra weight you've been meaning to deal with for years. So you walk into the local gym. The trainer greets you and asks what brought you in. You tell him your New Year's resolution is to lose fifteen pounds.

As you tour the gym, what do you think he's going to show you? He's going to highlight the excellent group classes they have. He'll bring you past the large area containing treadmills, exercise bikes, and other cardio-based machines. He'll tell you about the personal trainer program and the nutrition plans they can tailor for you.

What he likely won't dwell on is the basketball courts, the free weights, or the smoothie bar offering high-calorie protein shakes. And that makes sense, right? Because you told him your desire was to lose weight. You clearly communicated your pain and the trainer, in turn, showed you just how the gym could remove that pain from your life. As a consumer, this is what you want—a customized solution to your problem. Any response that doesn't work toward removing that pain is just noise, and it will push you away.

Over time, that gym owner might distill his ideal customers' pain points into three camps:

- One group wants to lose weight.
- Another group wants to gain muscle mass.
- The last group wants to do a blend of both, with a focus on generally improving their health and fitness.

Because it's the most moderate and widely applicable, the needs of the third group—those who want both more muscle and less weight—can be used to shape the default pathway I mentioned in an earlier chapter. If a lead doesn't clearly indicate their pain point, that's the track they'll start on for their customer journey. Those communications for this third (and default) customer will center around "If you join my gym, we're going to make sure you lose the weight you don't want and gain the muscle you need to live an energetic, healthy life. You're going to look and feel great." Who doesn't want that? This is also where you can let prospects know, "Tons of people just like you, who are living healthy, active lifestyles, have already joined our gym—you're in the right place!"

The information gathered in this step dictates the assets you are going to provide as you usher the prospect yet further along their customer journey. Doing this effectively requires the use of the ideal customer profiles that should have been constructed earlier.

Giving pain point segmentation the attention it deserves brings a wealth of benefits, such as the following:

- Improving overall customer experience significantly

- Shortening the time-to-purchase rate

- Enabling database segmentation around customer needs and desires

- Allowing for personalized suggestions based on what the customer themselves indicates they're interested in

- Providing metrics to track conversion and attribution rates

USE YOUR SUCCESS STORIES

Stage 2 is a prime example of how to use the success stories you've developed as social proof of how others, *just like your prospects*, who suffered from the same pain point have been transformed and no longer suffer. That strategy will speak directly to their reptilian brain, telling them that others in the tribe stepped into that great unknown and came out on the other side not just okay but better off. It is safe, it is good, and it improves our place in this world. Therefore, the reward outweighs the risk.

THE "JUST LIKE YOU" RESPONSE

I'll never forget spending Sundays visiting with my grandparents when I was a teenager. My grandfather was a golf fanatic, and that was always on TV. I remember the first time I heard the phrase "just like you" used in a commercial's voiceover that stated, "Great golfers, just like you, use XYZ brand of drivers on the course." That caught my attention; I'm not a great golfer, but I aspire to be. Many, many years later, that commercial and those words are still firmly in my memory.

We are all fickle beings. We feel that our pain is unique to us, and we fear that we suffer from problems differently than others do. We often feel embarrassment about this, and even shame. And yet the statistical data proves all of this to be wrong, so it's powerful to use our marketing communications to let prospects know they're not alone. That short, simple phrase of "just like you" conveys a host of crucial, comforting messages to those receiving it, according to noted expert Robert Cialdini, author of *Pre-suasion*.[17] It says:

- Whatever your problem, pain, objection, or desire, there are others out there having the same experience.

- We understand that experience, your experience, without you having to spell it out for us.

- Where you are in your journey is acceptable and normal.

- We know exactly how to eradicate your pain and get you what you desire because we've done it before.

---

17 Robert Cialdini, *Influence: The Psychology of Persuasion* (New York: Harper Business, 2021).

PAIN POINT SEGMENTATION IN ACTION

Built by Love worked with a financial education company that aimed to inspire people to invest in real estate and equip them with the knowledge to do so. When we hit Stage 2 while constructing their RAMP, the goal was to pinpoint the pains their customers wanted to overcome and to build out an understanding of the aspirational goal driving them toward real estate investing.

After examining the patterns that emerged from their current and former customers, it became clear that while all this company's ideal customers wanted to invest in real estate, there were several subsets with key differences in motivating factors, level of education, and challenges to overcome. This necessitated speaking to each subset group with a unique and tailored voice.

We found that a portion of this company's customers were seasoned investors who invest in real estate on a regular basis. It's their primary source of income, and they know the intricate details of investing. Rather than beginner-level how-to material, these investors are interested in the specific tool this company provides that gives accurate property appraisal details without requiring the customer to ever visit the property. This empowers a seasoned investor who professionally buys, sells, and leases real estate to profit from deals across the United States without needing to jet all over the country. The language present in the communications to this group, the material speaking to their specific pain points, the success stories, and the respective product highlights are worlds apart from the other pain point segmentations.

In contrast, the other primary pain point segment was found to be aspirational investors, those who wanted to quit their day job to invest in real estate. Their motivation was dissatisfaction with their current financial situation or job, and they saw real estate as the solution. To reach these people most effectively, the material had to be much more skewed toward what it's like to get into the industry. They needed language that speaks to their less developed level of real estate knowledge. And so, despite offering the same product to both segments, the language, the way the product was presented and highlighted, and the supporting success stories must look radically different.

As with the gym example, we then generated the third segment or the default pain point. This is a careful blend of the benefits, pains, and details from the other established groups. Having a hybrid option gives us a place to sort the person who fails to indicate which category they fall into. By presenting them some of everything, we have the best chance of showcasing something they will relate to that will then carry them further down the RAMP.

USING PAIN POINT DATA TO REFINE YOUR MARKETING

As with the ideal customer profiles you created earlier (Exercise 1), you want to narrow the pain points you're specifically targeting to two or maybe three things. That enables you to gain much deeper insights from your interactional data from customers and therefore generate more fact-based decisions to drive effective advertising and marketing campaigns, make better decisions with marketing spend, and ultimately, reduce the conversion timeline. Here are the questions you'll now be able to ask and the answers you'll now have:

- How many of the leads that opted in were segmented into pain point 1? How many of them were segmented into pain point 2? And how many were segmented into pain point 3? (As the prospects enter Stage 2, they'll either select their own pain point or be assigned the default pain point.)

- Knowing the total number of leads that came in and the numbers within each segmentation, look back at your ad sets. What population of people are being attracted by the copy and imagery?

- Then ask, how many of each segmentation converted from a prospect into a new customer? (We can now tie conversions directly to customer segments to understand what kind of person is buying.)

- From here, the next question can be asked: What pain point segment of new customers is driving the most revenue? And is this the same segmentation of new customers who make up the largest population of our new buyers? (Here is where the real gold lies. If a small population of our new customer segment is spending more money and worth more to the company, we now know precisely who our new ads, copy, lead magnets, and offers should be focused on. Conversely, the entire database that moves through Stage 2 will be automatically segmented so that we can make informed marketing and sales decisions by looking into our database and seeing what our entire population wants and needs.)

As you might see, with this amount of power being wielded at your fingertips and with an adept marketing team, you can create massive value within your company. Let's now get back to how this works.

USING PAIN POINTS TO MAKE REAL CONNECTIONS

Through the analytics available in today's digital world, it's easier than ever to see where people are clicking, what they're doing, and what content they're consuming. In an ideal world, this glut of data would help demystify marketing, further refining the communication you're providing on each specific customer journey.

However, the overabundance of information surrounding customer behavior seems to primarily create even more confusion for business owners and marketers. They may know a funnel or a specific offer is not performing well, yet they're still not sure what needs adjusting. The Marketing RAMP helps us zoom in to identify more accurately where the problem lies. Rather than knowing "something" is wrong with the engine generally, the RAMP reveals with precision the exact part that needs repair, saving us time and money and reducing missed opportunities with prospects and customers.

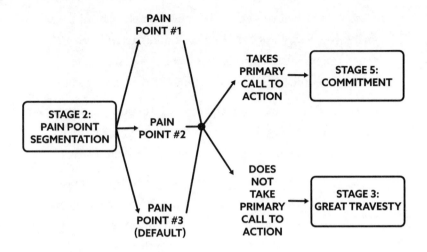

Figure 10.2. Stage 2: the process flow in your CRM.

Using the pain segmentation strategy within Stage 2—an early juncture of our new prospects—enables us to increase our conversion rates and reduce the time to purchase for those who are ready to buy now. Some may even jump directly to Stage 5: Commitment. But others won't be ready to buy—rightfully so, since they don't know us that well yet. Maybe they don't trust us, and maybe we haven't answered all their questions before they buy. These potential buyers will move into Stage 3: Tribal Alignment. The flow of work in your CRM is shown in Figure 10.2.

 TOP TAKEAWAYS

1. It's crucial to remember that, above all else, what motivates people to act is the avoidance or lessening of pain.

2. Building Stage 2 within your business is going to create a powerhouse of data that segments your database so you can make better-informed decisions on who your prospects and customers are and what they want.

3. Stage 2 will produce a critically important element of data, giving you clarity into whom your marketing and lead generation efforts are bringing forward, what segment is converting quickly, and what segment is the most valuable.

4. Once you know your ideal customer's pain point, tell them as clearly and concisely as possible how you're going to take away their pain. The simpler your messaging, the better.

5. Many times, people feel insecure and embarrassed about their pain and the associated strife it's causing them. Assure your ideal customers that the problems they're facing are normal, common, and you have the solution that can help them.

6. Once the ideal customer has been segmented into their specific pain point or (if they don't respond to your question) they are placed into the default pain point, you'll first tell them that they are in the right place.

7. Next, you'll show them success stories of people who have suffered from the same pain point as them and how that pain was removed by doing business with your company.

EXERCISE 7: STAGE 2: PAIN POINT SEGMENTATION

Here are the exercises you'll want to take to develop your company's Stage 2 of the Marketing RAMP. If you haven't completed the previous exercise, stop and go do it. It is not advised to skip steps, as you'll miss critical components in content, strategy, and communication necessary for the highest rate of success.

Identify the Primary and Default Pain Points

- Review who your ideal customers are and their pain points. Condense the pain points down to two or, at most, three categories of pain.

- Add one additional option that will be your default option. The default option is always an amalgamation of the other pain points. If the prospects moving through this stage fail to select their own pain point after a suggested delay of at least twenty-four hours, your automated marketing system can place them in the default pain point track.

Build Out Your Responses

Once a lead is connected to a pain point, build a response pathway with the following steps:

1. Acknowledge that they are not alone and that your company has helped solve that specific pain point for many people just like them.

2. Explain briefly how you can help them, and present the solution, which should be your primary call to action. The primary call to action is what you want them to do, such as buy a product or service or book an appointment.

3. Follow up with another communication that shows inspiring stories of others who suffered from their pain point but have now undergone a transformation and no longer suffer because they've chosen to do business with your company. You'll, of course, re-present the offer for them to act on your primary call to action.

4. If they are still hesitant to act, your third communication should be built around the following frequently asked question (FAQ) formula:

    a. List questions and answers on whom this can work for (this should be your ideal customer profiles).

    b. List questions and answers specifically from your ideal customer's pain points.

  c. List questions and answers from the ideal customer section of past possible bad experiences.

  d. List questions and answers from the ideal customer section of objections to the sale.

  e. List questions and answers about payment options.

  f. List questions and answers regarding any included guarantee or warranty after the sale.

CHAPTER 11

Stage 3: Tribal Alignment

The most effective way to unite mankind is a Great Travesty.

IF YOU'RE OLD ENOUGH, CAST YOUR mind back to a warm day in July 1985, when two billion people watched Freddie Mercury walk out on stage to sing "Bohemian Rhapsody" for one of the very last times. (And if you're not that old, check out the YouTube video.) It would go down in history as one of the greatest moments not only for the band Queen but also for the music industry as a whole. Musicians around the globe took part in the Live Aid event, putting on shows and raising $127 million for famine relief in Ethiopia.[18]

How did this come about? Why would the typically self-absorbed musicians of fortune and fame volunteer their time and efforts to this end? How was it that everyone from the humblest fan to Prince Charles and Princess Diana was there, watching, invested, and involved?

It was because they all saw the same images. Images of people starving; images of mothers, fathers, sons, and daughters—whole families—hurting in a way that was hard to comprehend. The Live Aid event

---

18 "Live Aid Concert Raises $127 Million for Famine Relief in Africa," *History*, July 12, 2021, https://www.history.com/this-day-in-history/live-aid-concert.

brought this Great Travesty to the world's attention. It took the global stage to show that people were dying horrible deaths and that it was their job to act.

Despite our species' many shortcomings, people feel moved to help others who are in their tribe. Plus, the event coordinators knew that people are more effectively motivated to act when there's a benefit in it for them, too. So people donated their money, and in return, they were treated to concerts by some of the greatest musicians of their time.

Throughout human history, it has been made abundantly clear that joining a tribe provides a greater chance for survival. From cave people banding together to forage and protect one another to modern-day nations creating alliances to fight their enemies, humans have always been driven together to fight perceived threats. In the Marketing RAMP, we call this tribal alignment, and it is our Stage 3 (see Figure 11.1).

This chapter and Exercise 8 are about how to build a tribe of loyal customers who identify your brand as the choice they stand behind. In the coming pages, you'll learn about how the Marketing RAMP organically aligns your customers and prospects to your brand by authentically and wholly convincing them that you have their best interests at heart.

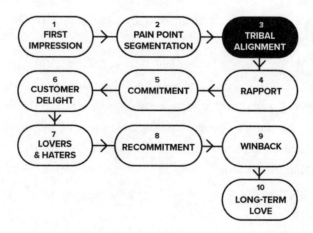

Figure 11.1. Stage 3 of the ten stages in the relationship journey: tribal alignment.

THE IMPORTANCE OF TRIBALISM

The need to unite with one another so that loss, pain, suffering, and threats are reduced by the power of the tribe is built into human DNA. It's so powerfully encoded in us that many of the actions we do daily show allegiance to the tribes we claim our association with, whether we realize it or not.

As you read the words that are printed in front of you, you are part of at least one hundred tribes.[19] Sound crazy to you? You're not alone! Many clients I explain this to feel the same way until I do this simple exercise with them. Answer these questions in your head, and you'll quickly see which tribes you're aligned to:

- What gender do you identify as?

- Are you married?

- Are you an Android or iPhone person?

- What's your favorite sports team?

- Do you believe in global warming?

- Do you eat meat?

- What religion are you?

- Are you a dog or a cat person?

- How do you view your country's current political system?

As you answered those questions in your head, I'm willing to bet some of them sparked strong emotional responses. Those kinds of emotions are what align like-minded people into their tribes. This alignment can be a catalyst for positive outcomes or used for great injustices, as we have seen throughout history. Understanding the power of human tribalism and using it in our marketing helps us begin

---

19 Cory J. Clark, Brittany S. Liu, Bo M. Winegard, and Peter H. Ditto, "Tribalism Is Human Nature," *Current Directions in Psychological Science* 28, no. 6 (2019): 587–592.

to move our prospect, our ideal customer, from observing our actions with caution to moving closer with curiosity. This matters a great deal. As discussed earlier, when the human brain is on the defense, the reptilian brain signals the presence of a threat, and the sympathetic nervous system triggers a set of responses preparing the body to fight or flee. This is what we want to avoid.

INCITING ACTION ONCE THE GREAT TRAVESTY IS EXPLAINED

As I talk about in Chapter 8, identifying a Great Travesty is critical in connecting with your ideal customers. And it's a good idea to reference that travesty in your first communications with prospects, starting with Stage 1. Here in Stage 3, you can follow up on your explanation of the Great Travesty by using one or more of the following three interwoven strategies:

1. Show prospects that other people just like them have succeeded because of us.

2. Give them a gift to take advantage of the law of human reciprocity.

3. Ask them directly to then take our primary call to action.

Let me talk about each of these strategies in more detail.

Others Have Succeeded because of Us

Whether or not you've used success stories as part of your Stage 1 or Stage 2 efforts, you definitely want to use any stories here that you can link to the Great Travesty. It is crucial to convey the message: "There are other people who believe this and care about this. It's not just you who thinks this is wrong. Everyone does, and we can work together to change it." You want to assure the prospect that they're not alone in how they're feeling. Instead, it's a collective unification around that travesty.

The goal here is to create a sense of ownership and togetherness that defines the tribe. It can't just be about making money. It's not just about providing goods or services. That's boring. Your customers won't care. At the basic level, there's nothing interesting about a business that seems likely to elicit customer care, so we must intentionally create what makes the human brain go, "I agree with that. I'm on their team."

Once the prospect has determined you are on their side and they're on yours, the defensive barrier goes down, and their brain shifts from expending energy trying to assess the perceived threat to listening to what you're saying. Aligning ourselves and creating connection in this way—making sure that our messaging can be heard—will result in a much higher chance that the customer has an ongoing business relationship with your brand.

Employ the Power of Reciprocity

An exchange of equal or similar value must exist in a relationship between two humans. If that trust is not formed, the relationship will dissolve. The exchange of value is one primary component that helps maintain the bond. Giving something of value to people you want in your tribe goes all the way back to our ancestors. In fact, it literally helped them survive. This act is still just as powerful today as it was hundreds of thousands of years ago. And, if you've been paying attention, you'll see how it's been built into every stage of the RAMP thus far.

The tribal alignment that begins to take shape after introducing the Great Travesty can be strengthened using the law of human reciprocity. It is a basic but powerful law of social psychology. Here's the gist: when you do something of perceived value for someone else, they are then inclined to return the favor. In its simplest form, if someone holds the door open for you, you're more likely to look back and hold the door open for the next person walking through. Why? Is it because you are a kind and generous person? Maybe. But it's also largely because your brain is wired in a way to return a favor because that ensures you are a team player within your tribe.

Giving a gift—or, in other words, providing the prospect tangible value—drives home the point that they really are on the right team. They are being rewarded for being on our side, and they see that immediately. We want them to return the favor by trusting us and stepping up to our primary call to action. This helps establish a deeper bond with our ideal customers. We've convinced them that we're actively attempting to improve their lives by living out our statement of the Great Travesty, and they believe us and are rewarded for it.

Think back to the Italian restaurant example from Chapter 9. Suppose the video says to a new lead, "If you are a person of discerning taste who is offended by the bland Americanized chains all around, come eat our uniquely authentic food," and it is paired with a 20 percent off coupon. The one-two punch of offering a solution to the Great Travesty and giving a gift to make that solution even more accessible is incredibly effective.

However, as powerful as the law of human reciprocity can be, it's important to give the gift along with the message that it's something you want the prospect to have whether or not they choose to do business with you. The gift will be perceived as disingenuous if it's linked to an aggressive push for the receiver to act on your primary call to action. We don't want our ideal customers to feel bullied or manipulated; we want them to understand that we're here to offer value to their lives, regardless of whether they give us money.

Asking Them to Take Action

Though you've likely included a CTA in other communications with prospects already, the prior stages are based on the principle that the prospect likely does not know you well enough or sufficiently trust you enough to make a purchase or to reach out and book a consultation. (Still, some prospects will be ready to act promptly, and that's why we always provide the option to buy or execute a CTA on every communication.)

By Stage 3, the odds are increasing that prospects are willing to act, so you have to ensure you have the right CTAs identified and featured in your Stage 3 communications. With this in mind, once we've addressed their pain points, we want to finish the arc. The idea we want to communicate is: "It's so easy to remove this pain from your life. Click here, do this simple thing today, and your pain will be gone tomorrow."

EXAMPLES OF TRIBAL ALIGNMENT IN THE WILD

While the tribal alignment facilitated by a Great Travesty is present in all successful brands to some degree, there are certain companies that have centered themselves around their travesty explicitly and entirely.

The shoe brand Toms comes to mind. They took the market by storm when they came onto the scene, highlighting how many impoverished people around the world lack shoes and emphasizing the many ways a lack of appropriate footwear can bring an added layer of struggle to an already hard life. The images they used, showing children walking miles to school in bare feet, tugged at the heartstrings of anyone who watched. Then, the clincher. For every pair of shoes purchased from Toms, a pair was donated to someone less fortunate—a beautiful business strategy hinged entirely on their Great Travesty.

Similar business models have been adopted across many companies. Warby Parker informed their target audience that many less fortunate people don't have access to glasses. They communicated the Great Travesty that not having access to vision correction makes basic tasks like reading words from a book, a computer screen, or a street sign nearly impossible. Lacking the resources to obtain eyewear greatly complicates daily life. The good news? If you buy a pair of Warby Parkers, they'll donate a pair to someone in need.

But let me make something clear. While it seems that social consciousness is on the rise in the business world—or at least the appearance of it, as consumers demand transparency and accountability—this isn't the only inroad to a compelling and successful Great Travesty.

Take Jeremy's Razors, for example. This company launched their brand with a nearly four-minute commercial that went viral as it directly pitted its brand against the "woke bullshit" it sees as taking over the world. It was irreverent, satirical even, as it made specific references to many cultural moments from the past few years. Their Great Travesty is that "big corporations don't care about you. They just care about being politically correct to the point of absurdity."[20] Jeremy's Razors, on the other hand, are for the everyman. They're speaking his language, and that language is common sense—or so they want you to believe.

THE POWER OF TRIBAL ALIGNMENT

Tribal alignment is powerful, and it's all around us. Think about the Green Bay Packers fans out in zero-degree weather with their Cheeseheads. They could be watching the game comfortably in their warm home, enjoying food and beverages of their choosing for free. Think about the people who would never dream of buying a piece of technology that wasn't from Apple. Think about the people who say, "Oh, I'm a Nike guy," or "I'm a BMW girl myself." Companies that create this sense of belonging and stoke the feelings of fandom create a community of people who are enthusiastic about the same thing to the point that it almost becomes a personality trait. Suddenly, what they're providing is so much larger than the service or product they're offering. It's becoming a subculture.

By the end of Stage 3, a percentage of the prospects moving through the RAMP will be ready to take our primary call to action and jump straight to Stage 5: Commitment. But the majority will need further convincing and will instead move along to Stage 4: Rapport. The flow in your CRM is shown in Figure 11.2.

20 DailyWire+, "Jeremy's Razors: The Greatest Commercial Ever," *YouTube*, March 22, 2022, https://youtu.be/s92UMJNjPIA.

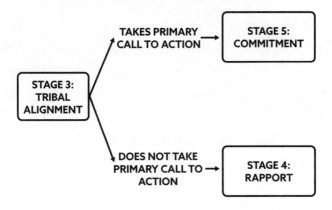

Figure 11.2. Stage 3: the process flow in your CRM.

   TOP TAKEAWAYS

1. People are wired to want the support and security that comes from belonging to a group of other people like them. For every situation, people crave and desire the protection of the pack except for two activities: finding a mate and copulation. Only during those times does a person seek to stand out from the pack, to be an individual.

2. One of the most powerful ways to create an alignment is to introduce a real or perceived threat that might amplify pain and create a loss of something valuable. This strategy, called the Great Travesty, within the Marketing RAMP is designed to create nearly instant tribal alignment with those who hear this message and are your true ideal customers. Once they are aligned with your tribe in support of preventing or fighting off this Great Travesty, they will listen to what you have to say and are more likely to act on what you're asking them to do.

3. As powerful as tribal alignment is, more must be done to ensure the recipient feels welcomed and believes that he or she is indeed

in the right tribe. We do this by presenting them with a gift of perceived value that should be tied back to the standard pains associated with this ideal customer base. Not only will you add value to their lives, but you'll also show again that your company is the expert and can solve their problems.

4. If you've built the entire Marketing RAMP to this point, your prospects will have moved through Stages 1 and 2 already. Therefore, this will be the second gift of perceived value you've given them. The first gift was given to them in Stage 1 as either being the lead magnet they've opted in for, or they came through the default track in which a gift is given in the first communication.

5. Adding value and providing gifts along the way of the relationship moves them closer to your brand and further from your competition. The law of reciprocity is also at play, showing that when we do something nice for someone, they will feel inclined to return the favor. We've been asking them along the way to take our primary call to action, but we have not been aggressive about it. As we move them into Stage 4, we will begin to make some withdrawals from that relationship bank account we've been building up to this point. The withdrawals will be directed at asking them to act on the primary call to action.

EXERCISE 8: STAGE 3: USING THE GREAT TRAVESTY FOR TRIBAL ALIGNMENT

Here are the exercises you'll want to complete to develop your company's Stage 3 of the Marketing RAMP. Make sure you have finished the previous exercises before beginning on this one, especially Exercise 5, where you developed your Great Travesty statements. Uniting your ideal customers around the Great Travesty is a very effective approach for tribal alignment.

- In any contacts with prospects, mention how you are solving this Great Travesty. (You should be able to find useful language in the work you did in the brand voice in the customer alignment section. You can also use highlights from the brand pitch in the brand narrative section.)

- Finish a statement with how the solution rights their wrongs. (This can be found in the ideal customer in the interests section.)

CHAPTER 12

Stage 4: Rapport

If you don't eliminate their internal objections,
your ideal customers won't buy.

I WAS SMITTEN WITH MY WIFE from the moment I laid eyes on her. I knew I needed to talk to her, so I walked right up and found a commonality to begin a conversation. I had to build rapport, or the relationship would go no further.

I kept things light and upbeat in the beginning, talking about our shared hobbies and interests. I offered a gift: "Can I buy you a drink?" By the end of the evening, I asked her on a date. In essence, I asked for more of her time and attention. I thought she was worth it, and she clearly thought the same about me because she said yes.

As you can probably tell, since I used the word "wife," my rapport-building was successful. Our relationship progressed, and our trust and affection for one another grew. But we knew we had to make sure our values were aligned before we took things any further. Did we share the same core principles? Did we want the same things? We talked it all through, articulating our life beliefs and expectations for the future and for our partnership. Only then did I move us to Stage 5: Commitment by asking my wife to marry me. Only then did she truly say yes. But it all began with a successful attempt to build rapport.

Back to business. In Stage 1, we welcomed our ideal customers with a warm greeting. In Stage 2, we promised to remove their pain, showing proof of how we have helped others. In Stage 3, we showed them the safety and community that can be found in our tribe, clinching the message by offering a gift.

Now, in Stage 4, we must ensure that the foundation we've laid remains firmly in place as we continue to provide additional value (see Figure 12.1). The rapport stage is designed to mimic the process that people follow as they actively choose to invest in and forge a bond with another human, just as I did with my wife and just as you have done with anyone in your life who holds great value to you. In this section of the RAMP, you define a templated cadence of how and when to communicate with prospects who have moved past tribal alignment. This ensures that you have the best possible chance of hearing a yes when you eventually do ask for their commitment.

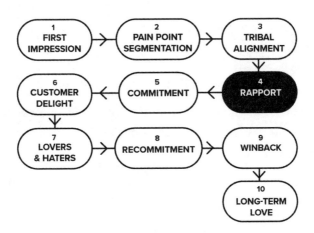

Figure 12.1. Stage 4 of the ten stages in the relationship journey: rapport.

By the end of this chapter and by using Exercise 9, you'll understand how to build a powerful rapport so that your ideal customers say yes to your proposal.

GOAL: STAY TOP OF MIND

During this stage, the aim must be to stay top of mind, drive value, keep the prospect engaged, and prompt them to act. We can't revert to a rapid-fire, generic sales funnel approach. We want to keep the content aspirational, informative, and centered around their pain points, continually presenting our offer but never in an aggressive tone. There should be value in every single communication being sent out. Tips, articles, videos, success stories, and other creative assets can be used very effectively here.

For example, if you are trying to convince your prospect to buy trail running shoes, you might send them an article about someone who just made an awesome thirty-mile trail run in the Rocky Mountains. Use photos that highlight the beautiful scenery and their smiling faces. Your prospect may never go on that specific run, or live anywhere nearby, but the good feelings the article creates in them might be all it takes to buy the shoes and hit their local trail.

Our goal in doing this is threefold:

1. To galvanize those sitting on the fence to action

2. To encourage those who enjoy our content but are not yet ready to buy to stay within our communications, and to make them feel safe and welcome doing so

3. To call others, the ghosts who are not interested in buying or hearing from us, to leave

FUNDAMENTALS OF THE RAPPORT STAGE

If someone ends up in the rapport stage, it's for one of three primary reasons:

1. Their internal objections haven't been satisfactorily addressed yet.

2. The time isn't right for them to buy, so we need to be patient.

3. They don't trust us yet. (Timing matters more than many marketers seem to realize.)

Actually, there is a fourth reason prospects can end up in this stage: because they are not your ideal customer. Don't fret; we've got a plan for these people, too.

To combat these issues, there are four primary strategies used in Stage 4 of the Marketing RAMP:

1. Reinforce trust by continuing to give real value, just as you've done in previous stages.

2. Provide social proof that others just like them have found success with your solution.

3. Eliminate internal objections and perceived purchase risk.

4. Continue communication throughout the average sales cycle.

The second and third strategies are where the success stories you've been developing come into play in a big and important way. Through the rapport-building process, you can use success stories to attack each of your prospects' internal objections and answer every question they may have. Being exposed to success stories being told by people just like them—people who had the same pain points but don't any longer, thanks to you—is an incredibly powerful tool.

ESTABLISHING A PACE OF COMMUNICATION

While rapport can happen quickly, often it takes repeated contact as the relationship builds over time. How long will that be? A rapport stage varies in length according to the timeline of when the largest percentage

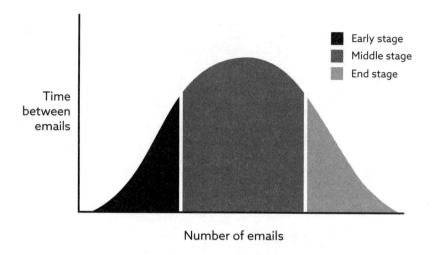

Figure 12.2. Bell curve representing time and cadence of marketing emails.

of customers buy. But we don't want to extend it beyond the maximum duration and risk adding to a consumer's marketing baggage. This means that communication cadence is an essential factor in the rapport stage and should resemble a bell curve (see Figure 12.2).

In the beginning, our outreach will come more rapidly, and we will wait fewer days in between each communication. As a prospect moves from the start of Stage 4 toward the middle, we slow down the pace. If they have not yet purchased, we don't want to agitate them by continuing an aggressive communication cadence. However, as they begin to enter the latter half of Stage 4, we shorten the days between our communications once again, as this ideal customer is now approaching a higher statistical probability of not purchasing from us.

You need to decide on your company's Stage 4 duration. It cannot and should not drag on indefinitely. The formula I recommend is:

Your average sales cycle = Number of days in your rapport stage

Truly, that's it. You want your Stage 4 to be as close as reasonably possible to the average time it takes a prospect to become a customer.

That said, the rapport stage is most effective when it's between thirty and one hundred twenty days, so if your sales cycle falls on either side of the suggested minimum or maximum duration, it's best to round it to one of those figures.

WHEN RAPPORT DELIVERS ON ALL ANGLES

What does this look like in practice? A successful chiropractic practice launched a consulting business to serve other chiropractors who were focused on implementing a systemized process to attract new patients, delight existing patients, and encourage repeat visits—all of which is crucial, as most chiropractors struggle to get people to schedule regular visits.

This business's Stage 4 needed to recognize that its prospective clients (other chiropractors) were hesitant to invest in a system for their sales and marketing. Many had never bothered with organized marketing before, and those who had were underwhelmed with the results. Still others had been in the field for decades and saw no reason to change their approach. Thus, the Stage 4 plan needed to attack all objections, in order of precedence and according to the ideal duration. It was crucial these chiropractors understood that this system was developed by one of their own, someone who understands the ins and outs of the industry.

Their rapport plan was built around the strategies mentioned earlier in this chapter: continuing to provide value, providing social proof, eliminating internal objections, reducing perceived risk, and continuing communication. In a first email, the business spelled out the Great Travesty that many chiropractors are not able to fulfill their mission of helping people simply because of logistics and missed connections. There was also a link to an informative article about how chiropractic clients don't seek help until they have been in pain for some time, so chiropractors should be educating their potential clientele on how to *prevent* pain through chiropractic treatment.

The next emails built rapport by touching on a common problem in the industry—imposter syndrome, the constant feeling of not having time to get everything done—and mentioning other common experiences that bond practitioners in the field. Throughout, they included a steady stream of success stories focused on issues representative of the ideal customer profiles this business was targeting. Taken all together, this communication plan was an incredibly effective stage that moved chiropractors from being mildly interested, at best, to believing that this system was the right pathway to reach their goals and help more people.

Stage 4 for this chiropractic business delivered on all angles, driving the prospects into the core call to action (in this case, a consultation). The robust rapport sequence did such a strong job of education through case studies that the sales process was made easier and the time to close was reduced. A win across the board.

FISH OR CUT BAIT?

Remember, at the beginning of this chapter, I mention there is a fourth reason why people enter this stage—because they aren't your ideal customer. Here, we call these people out and ask them to self-remove. The reason why we want them to remove themselves is that we want to ensure we have database hygiene and we are cleaning out the population of people who shouldn't be in the tribe. It'll save us time, money, and our reputation by excluding them from future communications. Unless, of course, they choose to stay.

If you reach the end of your maximum duration timeline without eliciting a response from the prospect, it's worth sending one final email along the lines of: "If we're missing a question that you need answered, please let us know. If you're enjoying the stories and tips we've been sharing but you're not ready to buy, that's perfectly fine. Stick around. Otherwise, if you're not interested in what we have to offer, please opt out of further communications because we don't want to bug you." The subtext of that final email in the rapport sequence is basically: "Are you giving up on [insert pain point]?"

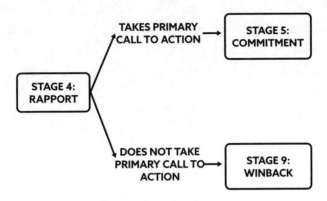

Figure 12.3. Stage 4: the process flow in your CRM.

We've been building up to this specific communication and, ideally, not many people are receiving it because they've accepted the call to action that we've been carefully guiding them toward. They will move on to Stage 5.

To those who are left, however, it's best to be respectful yet blunt. If a prospect does nothing (i.e., not opting out) in response to the final rapport communication, they are moved from Stage 4 into Stage 9: Winback. Those who step up and take our call to action progress directly to Stage 5: Commitment. The flow in your CRM is shown in Figure 12.3.

 TOP TAKEAWAYS

1. All relationships, whether they be intimate, friendship, professional, or with a brand, must have an exchange of value. At worst, the value exchange in the relationship is perceived by both parties as equal. At best, the consumer believes he or she is receiving greater value from the relationship than what they have

put in. This is ideally where you want your product or service to be. In any other case where an imbalance of value exists because the customer feels they put in more than they received in return, the relationship will dissolve, and negative emotions will surface from the dissolution.

2. If someone ends up in the rapport stage, it's for one of four primary reasons:

    a. Their internal objections haven't been satisfactorily addressed yet.

    b. The time isn't right for them to buy, so we need to be patient.

    c. They don't trust us yet.

    d. They are not our ideal customer.

3. The rapport stage's goal is to:

    a. Reinforce trust by giving real value

    b. Provide social proof that others just like them have found success with your solution

    c. Eliminate internal objections and perceived purchase risk

    d. Continue communication throughout the average sales cycle

4. To determine the length of your own Stage 4, use the formula I recommend: Your average sales cycle = Number of days in your rapport stage.

5. Of the many ways success stories can be employed to great avail throughout the RAMP, they are perhaps most key in building rapport.

EXERCISE 9: STAGE 4: RAPPORT

Here are the exercises you'll want to complete to develop your company's Stage 4 of the Marketing RAMP.

Determine the Target Number of Days for Your Stage 4

Use the formula given in the chapter to calculate how long your Stage 4 should last.

Your average sales cycle = Number of days for Stage 4

- If your average sales cycle is thirty days or less, then your Stage 4 should be thirty days.

- If your sales cycle is longer than 120 days, you may want to cap Stage 4 at that number.

Keep Developing Appropriate Success Stories

The general format for a success story is covered in Chapter 8 and Exercise 5. You should review any success stories you already have or develop new ones to ensure they build rapport with your prospects.

Remember to dwell on the aspirational outcome that the customer is now living a better life after having found your solution. Have them encourage anyone hearing their story who is in a similar situation to act now. Have them assure listeners that they will be thankful they did.

Plan Out Your Communications

Your communications within Stage 4 should revolve around the following talk tracks:

- Eliminating internal objections (you should be able to determine these based on your ideal customer profiles)

- Sharing the success stories you've developed

- Providing real value along the way, not just continually asking them to act on your primary call to action (in between communications where you're asking them to act, layer in real value for them, whether that be tips, videos, free resources, or anything that can help them move forward in their path to purchase)

Use the following in your final few communications:

- In your second-to-last communication in the rapport stage, call them out and tell them you've provided a lot of information to help them make an informed decision, but they haven't taken action. Ask them what they need or what is holding them back from acting.

- The last communication in this stage directly asks them if they are giving up on resolving their pain point. Give them the option to remove themselves from your communications if they are no longer interested. But let those who enjoy your content and services (but are not ready to buy) know that they are welcome to stay.

- For those who have not opted out and have taken no action, they will be dynamically removed from Stage 4 into Stage 9: Winback.

CHAPTER 13

Stage 5: Commitment

A sale is not a simple transaction. It's a commitment and the beginning of a deepened relationship with your ideal customer.

THERE WAS A TIME WHEN I LOVED WEDDINGS—and then I got married. Don't get me wrong. My wedding was wonderful, but I had no idea how much work went into planning one. Before, I simply knew they were fun—great people coming together to share a special moment, good food, music, drinks, and dancing. After, I knew just how many options there are and how many decisions and things to do pile up before the big day. Fortunately, our wedding was magical, and everything went according to plan. But my wife and I headed off to our honeymoon completely exhausted.

As I was still working out the final details of the Marketing RAMP at that time, I thought this example couldn't be more poignant for what your customers are likely going through as they enter your Stage 5, which is all about commitment (see Figure 13.1). We should understand not only what their journey has been like to that point but also how we can make it as positive an experience as possible.

In the earliest pages of this book, I lay out the five stages humans work through as they move from a noncommittal state to a committed

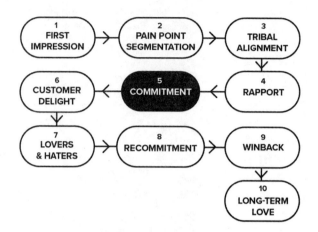

Figure 13.1. Stage 5 of the ten stages in the relationship journey: commitment.

state and explain that the first five stages of the Marketing RAMP are crafted to mimic this natural progression. Finally, now, the time has come for a formal commitment. As a company, we've invested a lot into arriving at this moment, and it's important that we don't lose steam at such a critical juncture. How to make that happen is the subject of this chapter and Exercise 10.

THE PROSPECT'S PERSPECTIVE

According to the *Oxford Dictionary*, "commitment" is defined as "a promise to do something or behave in a particular way."[21] However, it's also defined as "an engagement or obligation that restricts freedom of action."[22]

I named this portion of the Marketing RAMP the commitment stage for a specific reason. No word better describes the fullness of what

---

21 *Oxford Learner's Dictionaries*, s.v. "commitment," https://www.oxfordlearnersdictionaries.com/us/definition/english/commitment.

22 Word Hippo, "What Is Another Word for Commitment?," accessed March 31, 2023, https://www.wordhippo.com/what-is-another-word-for-commitment.html.

takes place in this stage. When customers choose to do business with you, they're choosing not to do it somewhere else. They are committing their money, their aspirations, and their belief that your company will make their life better. They've linked a part of their fate to yours, and that is a major role that your company is now responsible for delivering on.

Commitment can be shaped by many factors and motivations. I remember vividly the time I was rock climbing with my friends in Yosemite National Park. We had picked an easy route up Half Dome, a towering granite slab jutting thousands of feet into the sky. For me, an avid adventurer and lover of nature, it was as good as it got.

Until it wasn't. We had gotten off track, and we were lost a few thousand feet off the valley floor. There were no more anchors for us to fasten our ropes to on the rock face, and climbing down was impossible. The only way out of this situation was to go up. We had committed to the climb, and there was no option but to see it through.

From that point, we had to simul-climb. Simul-climbing is when each person is tied to the others by rope. If one person falls, they yell, "falling," and the others brace as best as they can to help stop the person's fall while hoping they, too, don't get pulled off the mountain by the momentum. It's an imperfect solution to a problem, and it's used when no other viable options exist. Each person is protecting the others' lives while simultaneously aware that they could very well be responsible for their deaths should they fall, pulling everyone off the mountain with them.

We all made it safely back to flat ground, thankfully. But I walked away from that experience with a newfound understanding of the power and consequences of making a commitment and seeing it through.

As business owners and marketers, we are too often desensitized to the level of commitment our ideal customers may feel when choosing to buy our product or service. Their pain, their joy, perhaps even their very life will be dictated by making that commitment to your brand. This is something that should not be taken lightly. It is our job to engineer the best possible outcome for them once they make this commitment. No matter the price point or the product or service you offer, we should treat this moment with the gravity it warrants.

If that isn't motivation enough, consider this: the decision to commit to your company may not be life or death to that customer, but if you get it wrong enough times, it could very well be the death of your brand. The Marketing RAMP is here to help ensure that doesn't happen, protecting both you and the consumer.

In any healthy relationship, people must feel they are appreciated and valued. Since most of our decisions are made on an emotional basis first with logic coming after, how your customer feels about your company is crucial.

SERVICE-BASED VERSUS ECOMMERCE COMMITMENTS

The commitment stage can take many forms depending on the business: booking a consultation, scheduling an appointment, requesting a proposal, making a reservation, or purchasing a product. Regardless of exactly what it looks like, our ideal customer has committed their time to us, and time is a precious resource that is not renewable. We must take this seriously. Our goal in this stage is to ensure that their engagement—the wedding day with your brand, if you will—is proportionately memorable.

Most service-based businesses need to have a call, appointment, or consultation to discover what the prospect needs. The commitment phase starts when a prospect books a time for this. Immediately, our communication begins by congratulating them on taking the step, trying to establish a personal connection, and confirming the details of the meeting.

Until the meeting occurs, we maintain many touch points with the prospect with the intent of driving higher conversions, combatting competitors and the dreaded price matching, and supporting our sales efforts by again attacking internal objections.

Ideally, prospects will show up to their appointment, accept our solution, and commit to the sale. We count that as a deal won and move those customers on to Stage 6. Conversely, a deal is lost when the prospect has either declined the offer or, after a specified amount of time we determine in our sales process, they have gone noncommunicative and failed to act. Then, they're moved to Stage 9: Winback.

Stage 5 looks different for ecommerce businesses that do not require proposals, consults, or any review of the customer's needs before a sale takes place. In fact, for those brands, the majority of Stage 5 is likely already built and functioning for you. After a purchase has been made, a transaction receipt needs to be sent to the customer along with an estimated delivery date. At the same time, an automated task for fulfillment should go out to execute the order. That's it. All customers are then automatically moved to Stage 6 so that we can continue the communication after purchase to combat buyer's remorse.

AFTER THE "I DO"

We don't want what happens after a commitment to be too utilitarian. When a customer executes the CTA, too often what happens next is not particularly inspiring. After a consumer has opted into a website, bought a product, or booked a consultation, they're often routed to a static thank-you page or they get a generic email that says, "Here's your receipt. Shipping details are coming." That's not what we want, as this doesn't show to your newly committed ideal customers that you are any different from your competitors. Most marketing and sales do their best to entice a purchase, and then, once that purchase has been made, the true colors of the company leave you with an underwhelming experience. In turn, this begins to erode the relationship that the company invested so heavily in building up prior to the sale.

I worked with a husband-and-wife team running a successful health and wellness business that provided coaching programs for doctors, chiropractors, dietitians, and other health practitioners. These ideal customers were busy and important professionals who expected others to value their time. Additionally, the coaching program had quite a hefty price tag. Between these two considerations, it was crucial to curate a first-class experience for those who opted into the free consultation being offered.

We knew, by design, that the prospect would be presented with the offer to purchase in that consultation. So we had to get them ready to say yes. Their RAMP's Stage 5 framework provided the comprehensive strategy for doing just that. Immediately after scheduling a time, the prospect was sent a custom video from the founders to get them excited. Then they received a strategic string of communications starting with program details, pricing, and an overview of what the experience is like. This was followed by concerted attacks against all internal objections, which was then all supported by their success stories. The goal of the predesigned communications was for the prospect to show up to their consultation with zero unanswered questions.

This strategy resulted in a system designed for scale that enabled the founders' team to increase the number of consultations being conducted without worrying about gaps forming in the sales process. The communication cadence—the entire experience—had been thoughtfully mapped out, all the way down to automatic reminders for sales reps when the prospect was moving close to their maximum duration. This all provided rock-solid metrics to identify when and why certain prospects were failing to convert.

Ultimately, these efforts resulted in a system that maximized the sales team's time, as they weren't spending their calls explaining the service and how it worked. That had already been done for them by the marketing within Stage 5. Furthermore, the work in this stage led their customers to Stage 6: Customer Delight by educating them with relevant information at the right time. This systematically removed competitor consideration (because of the best-in-class experiences we designed) and ultimately generated more revenue for the company. The CRM flow is very straightforward (see Figure 13.2).

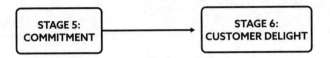

Figure 13.2. Stage 5: the process flow in your CRM.

 TOP TAKEAWAYS

1. The commitment stage is when your ideal customer has chosen to commit and act on your primary call to action. This is typically booking an appointment or consultation or when making a purchase.

2. A lot of time, effort, and money goes into getting a prospect ready to commit. It's an important moment to get right for your business. Equally, it's a big deal for a customer to commit to your brand and give you some of their finite resources. Thus, the moment should be treated with appropriate gravity and thoughtfulness.

3. If you are a service-based business, you'll want to ensure that the information leading up to an appointment (or quote) is designed in such a manner that it further educates the recipient and eliminates many basic questions that the sales team typically must answer.

4. If your business does appointments, proposals, or both, then Stage 5 is where you want all these communications to live. Appointment confirmations, reminders, and proposal stages (such as "proposal sent," "viewed," and "signed") all should reside within this stage.

5. If you are an ecommerce-based business, many of the transactional sequences have already taken place and therefore your focus must be on executing the best possible customer delight stage (Stage 6).

EXERCISE 10: STAGE 5: COMMITMENT

Here's a checklist to help guide you in developing your company's Stage 5: Commitment of the Marketing RAMP. Since this stage incorporates all three major departments—marketing, sales, and operations—it is important to have people from each area present for this exercise.

1. Outline how the sales team closes out the sale.

2. How is the new customer passed to fulfillment after the sale has been made?

3. Are there opportunities to streamline the sales-to-fulfillment transition with the primary goal of ensuring that your customer has a delightful experience?

4. Based on the steps in this exercise, create any associated tasks in this stage or a playbook to document the process.

5. Build internal communications that are automatically sent to the respective people or departments at each step in the handoff and during the fulfillment process.

6. Are there any items, communications, or tasks that your new customer must do before they can receive or consume what they purchased?

Service-Based Businesses

Here are the important things your Stage 5 should have if your business has consults or appointments before a sale is made:

1. Appointment or consult booked

2. Appointment reminders before the scheduled date:

   a. Deliver information about the services, price ranges, and what getting started will look like.

   b. Deliver success stories.

3. Once the proposal or quote has been presented:

    a. Follow up to see if they have questions.

    b. Deliver success stories that match the ideal customer's pain point.

    c. Present the process of what getting started will look like for them.

    d. You can reuse frequently asked questions (that we crafted back in Stage 4: Rapport).

4. Proposal signed or won:

    a. Handle any transactional things that must happen.

    b. Immediately move them to Stage 6: Customer Delight.

5. Proposal lost: Move them to Stage 9: Winback.

6. Prospect goes silent/stops responding: After a suitable time has passed, move them to Stage 9: Winback.

Ecommerce-Based Businesses

Let's cover the important things your Stage 5 should have after the purchase has been made:

1. Transaction receipt sent to the customer

2. Automated tasks for fulfillment to execute an order

3. Message to customers informing them of the expected delivery date

PART III

Cultivating Long-Term Love

ARE YOU GUILTY OF THINKING THAT once the sale is finalized, there's nothing left to do other than deliver that product or service to the customer? That's a common misunderstanding.

From the perspective of customers who made a purchase, the journey doesn't end until they have achieved their goals. And in fact, it may never end if you do a good job of continuing to cultivate the relationship and turn a one-time purchaser into a customer for life. Plus, you can't forget that there are many people who have just begun their relationship journey with your brand and have not yet made any commitment.

Dealing with customers who fit into these categories is the purpose behind the last five steps of the relationship journey (see Figure III.1). You want to increase the odds that people who purchased from you

Figure III.1. The last five stages of the relationship journey.

once will do so again and get those who have not made a commitment to either do so or self-select out of your system. Becoming empowered with this knowledge will make you well equipped to outperform your competition in these valuable and critical stages of the customer's journey with your brand. In the next four chapters, I walk you through the final five stages of the relationship journey.

CHAPTER 14

Stage 6: Customer Delight

Sixty percent of all buyers experience remorse after the purchase. Customers who don't feel good about their purchase won't buy again, or worse, they'll ask for a refund.

LET ME TELL YOU THE TRUE story of a boy and his stuffed giraffe. After getting home from a stay at the Ritz-Carlton in Florida, a little boy told his parents that his favorite stuffed giraffe had been left behind. The resort was contacted, the stuffed animal found, and a package was put in the mail to the family—but not before the staff did one game-changing thing.

They took the stuffed giraffe and made a story of what he did while he was away from the little boy. They took photos of it lying by the pool, getting a massage, driving a golf cart, and helping hotel security. He was even issued a hotel security badge. The staff wanted his owner to know exactly what the giraffe had been doing while not by his side. The effort they put into the package delighted the boy. But, more importantly, from a marketing perspective, the effort delighted his parents.[23]

---

23 Chris Hurn, "Stuffed Giraffe Shows What Customer Service Is All About," *Huffpost*, May 17, 2012, https://www.huffpost.com/entry/stuffed-giraffe-shows-wha_b_1524038.

This episode is a perfect example of what has made Ritz-Carlton the gold standard of customer delight. In an industry where options abound and the competition is fighting to cut prices on all fronts, Ritz-Carlton—a premier-priced luxury hotelier—is able to keep its hefty price tags while increasing perks, wowing with amenities, and creating true delight for their customers, who will almost surely be clients for life, just like the family of the little boy and the stuffed giraffe.

Now let me tell you about the opposite of delight. Remember that story from Chapter 10 about the car my wife bought? Despite having found the best solution to her pain point, immediately afterward she experienced doubt that she had made the best decision. That skepticism stewed inside of her. A few days after we brought the new car home, I said, "Hey, use your app to heat up the car before we go outside. It's cold this morning." She snapped back, "I don't know how. I really don't like this car. The dealership took advantage of me."

While the dealership didn't wrong her—they gave her a fair price and a good product—they made three critical mistakes:

- They failed to educate her on how to fully utilize and enjoy their product.

- They never followed up to see how it was going.

- They failed to infuse a single point of customer delight into the process.

My wife still doesn't know how to use most of the car's features—but you know what she gets via email every few weeks? Solicitations from the dealer, trying to sell her accessories to the car they never ensured she was enjoying. Talk about adding insult to injury. Recently, a neighbor walked by our driveway one morning and asked about the car and her experience with it because he was thinking about buying one for his family. What do you think my wife had to say? Although the car itself, in my opinion, is fantastic, her experience was not. And therefore, her internal talk track, her lens of the experience and therefore of the product, was negative. She told the neighbor she wasn't a fan, and she would recommend going with another car company.

That car dealership will never know they lost a sale for their top-of-the-line SUV that likely had the highest profit margin out of their product portfolio. They also don't know that they're going to have one less repeat buyer. And they are going to end up losing millions in sales to competitors that do understand the strategies needed to secure customer loyalty.

It's for this reason that Stage 6 of the relationship journey, customer delight (see Figure 14.1), is designed to make sure that how your customer feels about your company is positive and that it stays that way.

Stage 6: Customer Delight is about creating small, consistent moments of enjoyment and pleasure. These are the thoughtful touches that, even if minor, make an undeniable impact. Not only does infusing customer delight into the process offset any negative experiences a customer might have had with your brand, but it also reinforces positive interactions.

By the end of this chapter and by using Exercise 11, you'll understand the importance of continuing to sell your customer on what they've just purchased from you, even after the sale. We explore the reality of buyer's

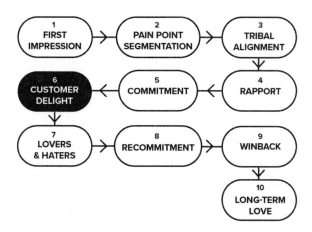

Figure 14.1. Stage 6 of the ten stages in the relationship journey: customer delight.

remorse and discuss how to eliminate that from your customers' experience. Finally, we dive into how you can engineer an after-purchase customer experience that infuses delight and creates a strong bond with your brand.

THE VALUE OF CUSTOMER COMMITMENT

Following up after a sale is what builds customer loyalty. It's a key moment to take advantage of. If your business is employing customer delight correctly, you will see a growing number of customers who love your brand. They'll return again and again. They'll provide word-of-mouth marketing. And because you've built a personal connection, they'll be more understanding if anything goes wrong or takes longer than expected. It is absolutely invaluable to have supporters like that out there who love you, who promote you happily, and who are patient when something goes awry.

But even beyond all of that, there is another huge business incentive to prioritizing customer delight: it's much less expensive to resell to an existing customer than it is to acquire a new customer. Obviously, when you try to acquire a new customer, you've got to find them. This requires continually appealing for their attention until they eventually opt in. Once they do, you're starting the customer journey from scratch. You've got to build and develop an entire relationship. You must work through their internal objections. It's a very long process, and it's an expensive process.

Think about it like this: once a customer has bought from you, they've already had their internal objections diminished, they've made a commitment to you, and they're in a late stage of their customer journey. Do you want to have to walk that entire distance from Stage 1 with someone new to get another sale? Or would you rather have somebody who pops back in right at the end, already knowing the value of your company and trusting that you have what they need?

Let's put figures to it. The odds of selling to an existing customer who is happy with their experience soon after the point of purchase are between 60 and 70 percent. Your odds of selling to a brand-new prospect, a new lead, or a stranger are between 5 and 20 percent.[24] Diving beneath this surface-level statistic, the cost of getting a repeat sale from an existing customer is nominal compared to the cost of acquiring a new customer. Studies show that it is anywhere between five and twenty-five times more expensive to acquire a new customer than retain an existing one.[25] That's why it's incredibly expensive and ill advised to rely on new customer acquisition for growth unless you have an arsenal of venture-backed money that isn't focused on your business being profitable or breaking even.

Instead, attention should be invested in repeat purchases from existing, happy customers, as well as earned revenue (the term for revenue brought in from existing customers who are referring others to your business). Getting that earned revenue figure as high as possible can only be achieved by having a great product, sure, but also by placing a high priority on infusing customer delight into the experience, even after the purchase.

THE SPECTER OF BUYER'S REMORSE

As mentioned before, conservatively, a staggering 60 percent of consumers experience buyer's remorse after a purchase.[26] Let that sink in. Six out of every ten of your customers experience regret after buying from you.

I experienced this recently while out to dinner. I was waffling between the stuffed salmon or the bison steak. I ordered the salmon, and then minutes later I watched as a glorious bison steak was set down at the table next to mine. I instantly regretted not ordering it. When my dish came, it was good. But it wasn't the steak. My mind's internal talk track

24 Jill Griffin, *Customer Loyalty: How to Earn It, How to Keep It* (San Francisco: Jossey-Bass, 2022).

25 Amy Gallo, "The Value of Keeping the Right Customers," *Harvard Business Review*, October 29, 2014, https://hbr.org/2014/10/the-value-of-keeping-the-right-customers.

26 Richard Laycock and Catherine Choi, "Black Friday Statistics, 2022," *Finder*, November 7, 2022, https://www.finder.com/black-friday-statistics.

took a negative turn: *The mashed potatoes are grainy, and the fish is dry, I think. Yeah, it is. Hey, why has it taken the waiter so long to ask if I'd like another glass of wine? The entrees do seem a bit overpriced. We should put this restaurant on hold for future date nights.*

All of that because of what? Buyer's remorse.

As a professional marketer, I was aware of what was taking place, and I corrected my internal dialogue. But for most people, once that runaway train of thought starts, there's no stopping it. The customer walks out and never comes back, while the poor restaurateur remains oblivious to all that has taken place.

Here's what's even scarier about buyer's remorse: most customers who experience it will not tell you! What they do instead is silently judge every subsequent interaction with your brand as their internal voices ask: Did I buy the right thing? Is this going to work? Is this worth the money? What about that other brand I was considering? They begin to stack reasons why they don't like what they purchased, and what happens next can be catastrophic to your chances of gaining a repeat purchase or converting this customer into a raving and loyal fan.

The prevalence of buyer's remorse is one reason why marketing teams sit awestruck as reports come in that repeat sales are lackluster and why the customer service department continues to receive complaints. More money is spent—and wasted—on what's wrong. Surveys go out, new messaging is changed, marketing starts mentioning that more dialogue needs to happen about the features of the products, sales begins to get blamed, and then advertising. A circular hell of insanity ensues, and no one comes out unscathed.

Yet too many brands are unable to recognize what's happening. They do their best to create a great product or service, invest in hiring the right people, and even perfect their advertising to lead new customers to the business. But they fail to see that once a sale has been made, things are just beginning, not ending. Whereas Stage 5 is about the execution of the sale and the transaction, Stage 6 is about the delivery, consumption, and engineering delight.

Buyer's remorse sets in immediately after the sale has been made. That's why you need to have a solid plan in place to follow up with a customer after the sale. If you don't, you are putting a lot of your potential repeat business at risk.

USING CUSTOMER DELIGHT TO PREVENT BUYER'S REMORSE

Before buyer's remorse sets in, we want to be there to immediately reassure the customer that, yes, they did make the right purchase. We want to tell them that they are smart and that their decision was a good one. We want to eliminate as much of the anxiety from the buying process as possible. If we're not doing that, then we're sinking back into the toxic sales and marketing culture the RAMP has been designed to replace.

We want to show them that our company is not about simply taking their money and then ditching them after the sale. If you do not step in to provide customer delight at this moment, you have a higher probability of a returned product, or worse, an unhappy customer who will complain about your brand. The customer delight stage attacks this head-on by infusing pleasure at the exact right moments, ensuring that a customer is feeling good about what they purchased and the people they purchased it from.

Infusing customer delight is not a one-and-done phenomenon. You can't focus just on the moment immediately after a sale. Your customer delight efforts should cover the entire timeline of your product's consumption (if the product is used up) or what it takes to help the buyer get proficient at using the product or service (like my wife and her new car).

Think about the activities and events that may need to happen once a sale is made for the buyer to achieve what they want to achieve. Then think about what you can do to make that transition from newbie to expert or satisfied user smoother and quicker. To get you started, I've summarized in Table 14.1 some factors that may affect post-sale delight of a customer.

TABLE 14.1. POST-SALE CUSTOMER DELIGHT

Post-sale consideration	Examples
The time it takes for your customer to receive what they purchased	Ordering clothes online and waiting a week for them to arrive (delayed gratification); buying a cold beverage at the vending machine (instant gratification)
The time it will take them to consume the product or service or get proficient in its use	A bottle of vitamins that lasts a month; an ice cream cone that is consumed in less than ten minutes; a monthly service that will last indefinitely; the days or weeks it can take to get up to speed in all the features of a new product
The learning curve needed to use or consume the product or service	The steep learning curve involved with buying a snowboard to go snowboarding for the first time; the instant mastery of buying and wearing a pair of sunglasses; learning to use a complex new financial software
How long it will take them to achieve the desired outcome	A weight-loss program that will take months for the consumer to reach their desired outcome; consuming a burrito from the local taco stand to fulfill their needs in a matter of minutes
Critical stages of consumption that your customers must pass through to have success	Signing up with a personal trainer and continuing to show up even when muscle soreness and fatigue happen as their body adjusts to the workouts
Stumbling blocks the customer may face	A software company's marketing team reports that new customers stop logging in after forty-five days, complaining that the software is too difficult; this says there is at least one—and likely more than one—stumbling block within the first thirty days
Milestones where your data (or the customer's self-reporting) shows transformational state changes (significant points of success)	A homebuilder relays major milestones in the homebuyer's new home being constructed and shares in the celebration with the buyer

By breaking down the post-sales process in this way, you can more clearly see the opportunities to infuse delight into the immediate post-sale part of the customer's journey, specific to the exact moment they are experiencing.

For example, my firm had a client who helped women with a thirty-day cleanse, removing sugar from their diets. When we walked her through this exercise of examining what happens immediately post-sale, she realized there was a moment in the process with high potential for buyer's remorse. Between days three and seven, the women who had removed sugar from their diets would experience headaches, low energy, and irritability. This was a danger point where new customers might be tempted to quit and then request a refund. We wanted to make sure that her customers knew feeling sick was a good sign; it meant the detox was working.

We ended up creating and distributing a string of success stories where other women who went through the course and detoxed from sugar successfully talked about how, even though they had felt grumpy and achy throughout the process, they emerged feeling dramatically better. They slept better, drank less caffeine, were happier, and began to lose weight.

Additionally, we wrote copy that directly called out what these women were experiencing. Our communication to new customers said, "Are you feeling like crap right now? I hope so! That means your sugar detox is working and you're on your way to an incredible transformation."

Our client's brand voice was very much "real talk," and her tribe of customers loved her for it. No matter the business or the tone, all businesses must continue reminding their customers of the benefits, removal of pain, and the aspirational outcome coming their way throughout their entire consumption process.

FIND THE FUN IN CUSTOMER DELIGHT

Stage 6: Customer Delight of the RAMP opens an expansive range of options and calls for a certain level of creativity and fun.

In Chapter 4, I show the empathy map and spectrum of formality for a luxury dog day care and kennel. This company had a bold initiative to open one hundred additional locations and become the national leader in the luxury dog care space. They are the Ritz-Carlton of the booming doggy day care industry, and their pricing reflects this. Their broader goal is the purpose of a Marketing RAMP as a whole: to systematize their marketing, sales, and customer experience to ensure the brand was providing equally amazing service across every location. More specifically, immediately post-commitment, the goal was to give customers, both brand new and existing, an instant sense that this company was the right choice for them and their pet, and by far the best in the business.

We built what I characterize as white-glove treatment into every step of the Marketing RAMP, placing a high premium on customer delight. Upon signing their dog up, new customers receive a personal email from the founders explaining that they understand pets are part of the family and that at this doggy day care, they would be treated as such. It all begins with sending the customer a customized dog collar along with a message about how the collar was painstakingly designed by experts to ensure it is safe, hypoallergenic, and makes for easy, painless handling of the pet.

One of the reasons why we crafted such a detailed message is because luxury is all about the fine details. Sure, most doggy day care providers have their own custom collars, but few have bothered to think about the safety of that collar, if it irritates the dogs, and if it was designed with thought for the comfort of the animal. Since dogs are actual family members in this business ethos, that message was crucial to deliver, as it would be a separation point between our client's brand and their competitors. That gift was not all, however.

The next trigger in the Customer Delight Stage is to send a custom dog ID tag, mailed in a well-designed box to the owner's home. One side of the tag has the dog's name and the owner's contact info, while the other has the local doggy day care's branch and phone number. This way, if the dog were ever to get out and the owner was unreachable, the dog could simply be dropped off at the nearest day care location. This sent the message that whether a dog was actively checked in or not, the company was always there serving their customers and protecting their beloved canine family members. That is a key difference in best-in-class treatment.

The white-glove treatment didn't stop there. The RAMP-directed CRM also sent communications to the owner explaining the physical signs that indicate their pet had fun at day care, since pets aren't exactly able to tell you how their day was. We celebrated thirty-day anniversaries and even had a sales rep call the customer at that mark to ensure they were feeling the delight we were trying so hard to instill.

The level of detail infused into Stage 6 created predictable results and experiences that enabled the brand to continue expanding its luxury dog empire nationally, without sacrificing quality or customer experiences. It is this level of detail that is unearthed in the Marketing RAMP that builds more than a business. It builds an empire that can withstand the test of time and the assaults made by your competition. It is the details within that transform your customers into people who are in your tribe. They love you, and wherever you go, they're coming with you.

ACHIEVING MASTERY IN CUSTOMER DELIGHT

Let's briefly discuss another example of mastery in delivering customer delight: Disney World. Have you ever been there? If not, it's an expansive amusement park that takes most people days to fully explore. It is the world's number one most visited amusement park, with a staggering average of 58 million people passing through their gates annually.

For math lovers, that's an average of 158,904 per day.[27] That many people at an amusement park means you're going to be waiting in lines everywhere you go. Now, imagine if someone were to say to you, "I want you to pay an exorbitant amount of money to stand in line for six hours. In return, I'll give you sixty minutes of entertainment." You would laugh in their face.

And yet Disney is a growing multibillion-dollar company—and that is because they have perfected customer delight. Every part of the experience, from the moment the customer enters the park, as they wait in the extensively long lines for the amusement rides, through to leaving the park, has been designed to inspire good feelings and create aesthetic moments and memories that encourage them to return. It doesn't just appeal to kids. There are plenty of childless adults who go with their friends. When they look back at their photos, all they remember is the happiness. Most don't care about the cost or the physical weariness. Through careful strategy and placing a high priority on customer experience, Disney has created a tribe of loyal and passionate fans who will return for as long as they're able.

What's important to keep in mind, however, is that customer delight is no more the end of the customer's journey than is the initial purchase. As customers continue to use your product or service, you need to evaluate their experiences and determine which are your lovers and which are your haters. The flow in your CRM is shown in Figure 14.2.

Figure 14.2. Stage 6: the process flow in your CRM.

27 "Walt Disney World Statistics," *Magic Guide*, accessed March 9, 2023, https://magicguides.com/disney-world-statistics/.

TOP TAKEAWAYS

1. A customer's journey does not end at the moment of purchase. If that's where you stop interacting with them, you're essentially ditching them the second you've snatched their money.

2. Investing in a customer beyond the moment of sale is what builds lasting loyalty. It's cheaper and faster to resell to an existing customer than it is to woo a new prospect. Depending on which industry your business is in, studies show that it is anywhere between five and twenty-five times more expensive to acquire a new customer versus retaining an existing one.

3. Sixty percent of consumers experience buyer's remorse after making a purchase, which can morph into bitterness toward your brand if left unaddressed.

4. Infusing customer delight into the sales process helps combat this buyer's remorse, generally fostering positivity and helping secure repeat business.

5. Your customer delight stage should be built to last as long as it takes your average customer to fully consume your product or for them to become proficient at the use of your product or service. For example, if you sell a bottle of vitamins with thirty capsules inside and the daily recommended dosage is one capsule per day, your customer delight stage should be thirty days (and should be suggesting a refill by day twenty). If you're selling cars, your customer delight stage may last anywhere from a few days to a few months as you work to ensure the customer knows how to get the most out of the car's features.

6. Address stumbling blocks, your average churn, as well as pivotal moments of success that occur during your typical product consumption life cycle. Addressing these things will help your

customers overcome the challenges they face, and you can celebrate the small wins with them along the way.

7. If embraced, the customer delight stage of the RAMP enables your brand to really showcase its personality and creativity, winning people over in the micro-moments.

8. Once your customer has finished Stage 6, they should be automatically moved to Stage 7: Lovers and Haters.

EXERCISE 11: STAGE 6: CUSTOMER DELIGHT

Here are the exercises you'll want to complete to develop your company's next stage of the Marketing RAMP. It is not advised to skip steps, as you'll miss critical components in content, strategy, and communication necessary for the highest rate of success.

Identify What Your Customers Experience Immediately Post-sale

Think about the activities and events that may need to happen once a sale is made:

- After the sale, will it take time for your customer to receive what they purchased?

- Will consuming the product be fast (minutes or hours) or does it take time (days or weeks)?

- Is there a learning curve to the consumption of the product?

- Will they experience the desired outcome of the product quickly or will it take time?

- Are there critical stages of consumption that your customers must pass through to have success?

- Are there stumbling blocks along the consumption path?

- Are there milestones where your data (or the customer's self-reporting) shows transformational state changes (significant points of success)?

Identify a Target Duration for Your Stage 6

Duration for your Stage 6 should be at least the average duration for how long it takes to consume your product or service or become proficient in its use.

Identify Actions You Can Take to Increase Customer Delight

Review your answers to question 1. What are the key moments across the duration of Stage 6 where you can infuse points of delight for the customer? How?

- Typically, an infusion of delight happens right after purchase.
- If there are churn points, milestones, or challenges along the way, you'll want points of delight at those moments in time as well.

CHAPTER 15

Stage 7: Lovers and Haters

Knowing who loves you, who hates you, and who you're at risk of
losing is the magic of creating a higher customer lifetime value.

JAMES BOND IS ONE OF THE most successful multibillion-dollar action hero
franchises in the history of motion pictures, and this British secret agent
has something to teach us. Bond knew quite well the power of identifying
who in his world were his lovers or his haters, and who were at risk of
potentially doing him harm. No matter whether the person loved him
or was trying to harm him, he treated them all with the same manner of
respect. It was those who were at risk that had the ability to do him the
most damage, and those people were the ones that he always ended up
swaying to his side, who helped him to save the day and make it out alive.

The real world, especially in business, doesn't end that way. Many
times, customers who aren't overly happy or are discontent are ignored.
They are the ones who pose the greatest dangers to a business's survival.
We distill the differences between happy, unhappy, and at-risk customers
in this chapter, and we devise a plan that will ensure your business not
only lives to fight another day but wins the battle.

In Chapter 14, I describe how Stage 6: Customer Delight is all about
engineering a strategy to ensure your customers consume the product

or service they purchased from you and feel great doing so. But there is more that goes into post-purchase maintenance than customer delight. There is so much that can be done once a prospect becomes a customer to ensure they have a positive experience and cement their loyalty. This will refine your approach moving forward. Of course, what this looks like varies according to what your company does. But even large-ticket, hard-asset firms like home builders are making a massive mistake if they disengage with their buyers after the sale has been made.

No matter what, the goal is to have our customers love doing business with us regularly. That's the purpose of Stage 7: Lovers and Haters (see Figure 15.1).

In this chapter, I talk about how you need to ensure your brand is checking in with customers to gauge if those efforts are actually working. It's all about the importance of gathering feedback on how your customers feel about your company. The feedback collected can be used to identify problems with your product or service and improve the customer experience so you know what to sell next and to whom. It also works to develop a process that automatically generates referrals, success stories, and content for your advertising, sales, and marketing efforts. Keep those points in mind as you complete Exercise 12.

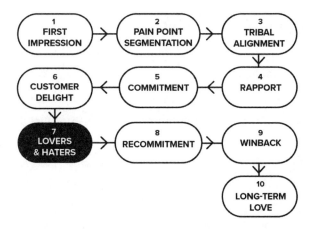

Figure 15.1. Stage 7 of the ten stages in the relationship journey: lovers and haters.

TABLE 15.1. CUSTOMER ATTITUDES AND MARKETING SEGMENTS

Customer's attitude	Marketing segment
Unhappy	Hater
Underwhelmed	At-risk
Happy	Lover

THE SEGMENTS: LOVERS, HATERS, AND AT-RISK CUSTOMERS

For the purposes of guiding your marketing strategies, it's helpful to segment your customers into three categories, as summarized in Table 15.1. Following the James Bond model, we need to know which customers are unhappy with us (the haters), those who are happy with us (the lovers), and those who fall between the extremes who could pose a risk to our business (the underwhelmed at-risk segment).

I've found that having three segments allows for enough customization in your responses without adding too much complexity to your systems.

GETTING CUSTOMER FEEDBACK

Inviting customers to rate their experience and being humble and open to really hearing what they have to say requires courage, but discomfort is where we grow and learn. Refusing to check in with customers hurts your business. The only way you can know what's working and what isn't is by asking. Some people think they can bypass that step by checking their sales figures. But sales can be a lagging indicator, especially at larger organizations or if you have a pipeline that you're working on. You need to ask the people you're selling to in order to know how your company is being perceived and how you can adjust. The information you learn will prove invaluable in the subsequent phase of the RAMP.

Yes, it stings to hear that people hate us, and it makes us feel good when we hear people love us. But it's important to know either way. Never assume that your customer is pleased with the experience they had with your company. We must ask, we must listen, and we must thoughtfully follow up. Humans need acknowledgment. That's an important part of a healthy relationship, which is something our Marketing RAMP delivers.

The lovers and haters stage is where we ask our clients to rate our performance and relationship. For maximum effect, gauging customer satisfaction needs to consist of more than simply collecting a numerical net promoter score (NPS). Infusing a personal element when gathering valuable data supports the entire RAMP approach and is crucial to cultivating and sustaining a business built on the foundation of love.

Before I dive into the details of how you want to segment and then classify your respondents, including those who don't respond, I think it's best we get the numerical ratings out of the way.

Most customer satisfaction surveys I have seen are based on a scale of 1 to 10, with option 1 usually being the lowest possible rating and 10 being the highest possible rating. Often, these ratings are weighted by 10 points, so the maximum score is 100 points, or 100 percent. If the recipient selects a rating of 5, that is weighted as 50 percent. A selection of 8 makes the score 80 percent, and so on. If you recall your grade school education, this matches perfectly to the typical grading scale in schools, by which 50 percent or less is an F, 60 percent is a D, 70 percent is a C, 80 percent is a B, and 90 percent is an A.

In theory, this approach works just fine, and it is easy to understand when people are rating your business. However, as discussed previously, presenting people with too many options is counterproductive. And when the subject is ratings, it turns out that people become more dissatisfied with a product or service when they make a rating choice, according to the research by psychology professor Barry Schwartz, author of *The Paradox of Choice*.[28] Not only do your recipients become more dissatisfied

---

28 Barry Schwartz, *The Paradox of Choice: Why More Is Less* (New York: Harper, 2005).

when presented with too many options, but also they statistically choose 7 as the default on a scale of 1 to 10. So how meaningful is that 7? And how can you determine the true difference between someone who rates you a 4 and someone else who gives you a 5? What does a 70 percent rating mean compared to an 80 percent rating? Arguably, you cannot decipher the true difference, and therefore, your exercise in getting customer satisfaction ratings is futile and an unnecessary friction point for your customers.

One December afternoon, as my team and I were wrapping up the year's work, we were reviewing our current and past client satisfaction ratings using the standard ten-point scale. No one could determine what was good, what was great, and where the line for improvement was. I had had enough, and that's when I demanded we do better than the industry standard and switch to a five-point scale. That was enough to get some differentiation between groups but not so much as to make it harder for customers. The link between these rating systems and the segments identified earlier is shown in Table 15.2.

The goal in asking customers where they fit on our rating scale is to gradually move everyone from the low end of the spectrum (those who are unhappy with us) to the opposite end of the spectrum (those who love us).

TABLE 15.2. RECOMMENDED RATING SCALE

Customer's attitude	Marketing segment	Rating	Description
Unhappy	Hater	1	Very dissatisfied
		2	Somewhat dissatisfied
Underwhelmed	At-risk	3	Neutral
		4	Somewhat satisfied
Happy	Lover	5	Very satisfied

Remember, it's always cheaper to generate sales from repeat customers than it is to acquire new customers.

IMPROVING RESPONSE RATES

Many businesses report low response rates to the surveys they send out. That is likely because without putting effort into ensuring customers had a pleasant and fulfilling experience, it is strange and inequitable to ask them to take their time providing feedback. We will likely be ignored, with the only people who bother to get back to us often being those at the extreme ends of the standard bell curve. These incredibly upset or incredibly happy people make up the minority of our actual customer base and don't provide particularly applicable or widely helpful feedback. Furthermore, it can be frustrating for customers who take the time to fill out a survey when they never hear from that company again. This happens all too often, and it certainly doesn't encourage them to bother responding to subsequent surveys.

MAKING A WITHDRAWAL FROM
THE RELATIONSHIP BANK

When it comes to marketing, every time you reach out to communicate with someone, you're either making a deposit in the relationship bank or you're making a withdrawal. You better make sure you've put enough money in that bank account through customer delight that you can afford to make a withdrawal by asking for a survey response. You don't want to bounce that check. Even with happy customers, asking them to fill out a survey is just that, an ask. We want to respect their time, acknowledge their contribution, and make sure we're providing reciprocal value throughout.

Keep It Simple

My strategy relies on micro-commitments from customers. If we pose too many questions at once, the investment of time we're asking for may turn potential respondents away. It's best to keep customer surveys simple and to the point. That means using the five-point scale I describe with the simple question "How would you rate your experience with us?" Or there are instances where we've gone even simpler and asked customers to self-select which one of three adjectives they identify with: unhappy, underwhelmed, or happy.

For example, clicking a link would then take the customer to a page that has only one question: *Which of these adjectives best describes your opinion of us: unhappy, underwhelmed, or happy?* (Or "rate us on a scale of 1 to 5.")

Explain How Their Contribution Will Benefit Them

The original communication with a customer—the one that will ask them to do the rating—should make it clear that there is a direct benefit for that person. Otherwise, the likelihood of them participating is greatly reduced. We need to let our customers know this is not just another automated survey. There is a real person or team that wants to hear from them.

Confirm You Are Paying Attention to All Responses

It also helps to explain why you want to hear from them and what you plan to do with this information. This communication might have copy along the lines of:

When you provide your valuable feedback:

- Every response is read, and we will respond individually to each person who provides feedback.

- If you're not completely happy, we are going to do our best to fix it.

- We use your input to help our company improve our [products or services] and solutions for you and valued customers just like you to move forward.

A video can be used to great avail on the survey page. For example, a sixty-second clip of the founder explaining, "We strive to deliver best-in-class products and customer experiences, and your decision to purchase our product is a vote of confidence in our brand that we deeply appreciate. We care if we lived up to your expectations, so your response to this simple survey would mean a great deal to us."

Slip In Some Follow-Up Questions!

After the customer completes the one-question survey, they can be taken to one of the three dedicated landing pages that have been set up for each segment. There, they will find several follow-up questions along with a video thanking them for their honest feedback and offering commentary that makes them feel acknowledged and heard and is specific to their satisfaction rating.

Having watched a follow-up video, the customer is likely more inclined to answer the additional set of questions, which run along the lines of: "Can you talk about the value of the product? Is there anybody from the team that you want to specifically call out? Any other feedback you want to give us?"

The respondent could still simply close out of this field, which is fine. We put our questions in order of priority and made sure to gather the most important piece of information first. However, if someone answers the first question, they've invested some of their time already. Human brains like to close the loop, and there's a good chance they'll continue forward with the extra questions. The information gleaned from these answers provides an extra layer of depth and richness to our understanding of why the customer gave the rating they did, how we should follow up with them, and what it means for the overall customer experience we are crafting.

DEVELOPING RESPONSE STRATEGIES

A multimillion-dollar toy company specializing in safe, nontoxic wooden toys as educational products reached out to my agency for assistance in creating direct channels of communication with their customers. More than 90 percent of their business was passing through Amazon and Etsy, and they hoped that implementing the Marketing RAMP would elevate their direct sales to reduce their reliance on third-party platforms.

To grow their customer base in a continually predictable manner, we needed to harness the power of their number one method of obtaining new customers: referrals. Many happy parents, grandparents, or other loved ones who purchased a toy for the child in their family were dazzled enough by the product that they organically wanted to talk about the experience. We wanted to encourage these lovers to keep it up and get other customers into that same lover category. We used the RAMP's Stage 7 to identify existing lovers and request testimonials while also extending an exclusive offer where referring the brand to friends or family would result in both parties getting a discount.

We also built out predesigned paths for customers who were only moderately happy with their purchase, as well as those who may have been unhappy. The RAMP flagged those instances and triggered a sequence of events we believed had the best possible chance to move them quickly and effectively toward the happy end of the spectrum. The result of this brand's robust Stage 7 was a continual flow of testimonials, success stories, referrals, and delighted customers who returned again and again to purchase more from the company. Within months, the business's reliance on third-party platforms was no longer a consideration, as their direct sales boomed.

This story illustrates the value of having a strategy in place—and captured in your RAMP—for dealing with the three segments of customers. Let me explain more about what went into this strategy.

Responding to the Haters and At-Risk Customers

There is significant overlap in what customers in the underwhelmed category and what customers in the unhappy category are likely feeling, and we don't want either group writing us reviews. Mediocre reviews from customers who feel neutral or underwhelmed drag a business down. It is important to devise a plan to reach out to customers who indicate they are in this segment. These people may be doing business with you simply because they don't have any other options or because it was the most convenient thing to do at the time. There is very little loyalty in this segment. Customers who are generally indifferent to your brand are likely to be swayed by a competitor, and you'll lose their business forever.

Ideally, the content of the specific landing pages that you'll direct people to can also be used as a vehicle to address the concerns of the unhappy customer swiftly and directly. Assure them that someone will contact them within the next business day to discuss their concerns and rectify any and all problems. As with the moment after the sale, this is a key point in the customer journey to personalize the process and try to set a positive tone.

After the survey is completed, some of our clients assign someone to call the unhappy or underwhelmed customers the very next business day. Others offer discounts, special packages, or a letter from the CEO. There are many effective strategies you can employ, but the micro-goal is to identify these people early to make sure you don't ask them to write you a review and so you can address their concerns before you try to sell to them again. The macro-goal is to transform mediocre experiences into amazing experiences so that your brand's reputation becomes an entity unto itself. Happy customers beget more happy customers.

I recognize that reaching out to all negative and neutral-reporting customers may not seem scalable, but I encourage you to find a way to make it happen. These people are a long way into the customer journey, already on Stage 7 of a ten-stage process. They've committed and purchased from your company. You can now learn from your customers and, if you're willing, hear where you've underwhelmed them. This will empower your organization to fill the gaps in the buyer's journey, improve internal processes, and save at-risk customers. Making the purchaser feel heard and gleaning valuable information in the process is a win-win. The feedback should then be compiled and shared among the departments and leadership team to help make future business decisions.

Can you really change a hater's mind? It depends. There is a small percentage of customers every business gets where, regardless of what you do, they will not be happy. They want more. They want free. They want it yesterday. Nothing will ever be right. The goal is not to try to change these people but to diffuse their anger. They might not be happy with you, and they likely won't be repeat customers, but they could be placated by the fact that someone cared enough to reach out and issue an apology. I'm not recommending that you give them their money back or offer free things. But I do believe you should find some way to issue a sincere apology, even if you weren't strictly in the wrong.

Maybe there are some haters who were genuinely provided subpar service. In these cases, you can adjust your messaging according to any specific insight they provided in the survey form, but the message will likely be along the lines of: "I understand we haven't delivered on our core values. What can we do to make this right for you?"

DUE DILIGENCE ON UNHAPPY
OR UNDERWHELMED CUSTOMERS

With both the haters and those that skew more neutral, it's important to do your due diligence before engaging in live interaction with them. Go look at their customer history in the CRM. Whom did they talk to? What did they buy? What was the process? It's important to know what their experience was like as much as possible so that you go into the conversation equipped to de-escalate the situation and don't further frustrate them.

Making the Most of Your Lovers

Fortunately, some customers are going to be deeply, wholly happy with what our company is doing. We'll call them the lovers. While we want to make sure to capitalize on their praise and request a testimonial, their landing page should contain a video that first thanks them for their support and loyalty. Then, we can request a testimonial. These are the people you want new leads to hear from. You can even give them the option to leave that review right there on the landing page.

The RAMP helps develop an automated process to do the following:

- Identify and capture success stories for use in advertising and marketing efforts.

- Highlight content for use on social media channels and websites.

- Continually add and update success stories available for use throughout the Marketing RAMP.

Regardless of whether a lover chooses to contribute a success story or not, this is also an opportune moment to introduce the idea that they can—and should—refer us to their friends, family, and colleagues. To sweeten the deal, I strongly suggest providing a reward of real value for such referrals from your brand's lovers.

NEXT STEPS

What should your RAMP do with customers once they have completed Stage 7? My advice for how to structure your CRM is shown in Figure 15.2.

- Haters: After trying to resolve their issues, you can opt to move them into Stage 9: Winback or move them to Stage 10: Long-Term Love.

- At-risk: After trying to provide more delight and thus move them into the lovers category, if they are still in the

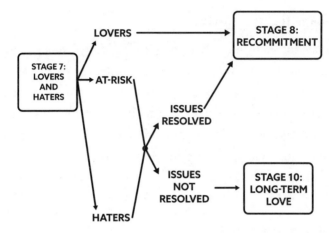

Figure 15.2. Stage 7: the process flow in your CRM.

at-risk category, you can opt to move them into Stage 8: Recommitment, where you sell them again, or you can move them into Stage 10: Long-Term Love.

- Lovers: After they have been asked to be a success story and educated on how to earn rewards for referring business to you, they are moved to Stage 8: Recommitment, where they will be sold to again.

 ## TOP TAKEAWAYS

1. It is unwise to assume customers are pleased with your business's performance without asking and humbly listening to whatever feedback comes your way.

2. Ideally, unhappy customers will move toward the positive end of the spectrum once they feel heard by you, and happy customers will be willing to contribute a success story.

3. The information—both positive and negative—gleaned from customer surveys carries immense value and can be used to improve your business in a wide variety of ways.

4. Your biggest population of current customers is likely your at-risk customers. These are the people who rate their satisfaction as "somewhat satisfied," which is a 4 on a five-point rating scale. Or they rate you as "neutral" or "neither dissatisfied nor satisfied," which is a 3 on the five-point rating scale. This population can and will be swayed by your competitors that offer lower rates, more benefits, or better features.

5. Without proactively developing a strategy that turns at-risk customers into lovers (who rate you 5 out of 5), you will be creating additional friction for them and giving your competition an opportunity to woo them away. If you are sending sales and marketing offers to those who rated you anything less than "neutral" or 3 out of 5 on the rating scale, you are doing more damage than good and creating a toxic relationship with customers when you should have been trying to resolve their dissatisfaction.

6. When you request feedback after their purchase, you must do the following:

   a. Communicate that there is a real person (or team) who wants to hear from them, not just another faceless survey that no one looks at.

   b. Tell them why you want to hear from them.

   c. Tell them what you are going to do with this information and how it will benefit them. (Remember: Asking them to do something is a withdrawal from the relationship bank account. You should show that this action redeposits value back in.)

   d. Send a video along with the request so that the customer can hear and see who is asking for this feedback. Again, this ties back to showing that you do want to hear from them and there is someone on the other side who will read it.

EXERCISE 12: STAGE 7: LOVERS AND HATERS

Here are the exercises you'll want to complete to develop your company's next stage of the Marketing RAMP for the highest rate of success for your business.

Update Your Requests for Feedback

Evaluate your feedback requests by the following criteria and make adjustments as necessary. Do you clearly do the following:

- Communicate that there is a real person (or team) that wants to hear from them, not just another faceless survey that no one looks at?

- Tell them why you want to hear from them?

- Explain what you are going to do with this information and how it will benefit them? Remember: Asking them to do something is a withdrawal from the relationship bank account. You should show that this action redeposits value back in.

- Use different media (email, video) as appropriate? It is always more delightful to send a video along with the request so that the customer can hear and see who is asking for this feedback. Again, this ties back to showing that you do want to hear from them and there is someone on the other side who will read it.

- Clearly explain the rating system (using the three adjectives or five-point scales)?

- Determine whether you will have bonus questions that are optional after the customer has provided their rating?

Segment the Respondents

In your CRM, segment the respondents based on their ratings. Each segment will have its own path (see next step).

- Segment 1: Haters—those who rated you as a 1 or 2 (or identified as "unhappy"). The goal will be damage control.

- Segment 2: At-risk—those who rated you a 3 or 4 (or identified as "underwhelmed"). The goal will be to move them into the lover category.

- Segment 3: Lovers—those who give you a 5 rating (or identified as "happy"). The goal will be to gather their success stories and to refer your business in exchange for rewards, discounts, or commissions.

Identify Follow-Up Actions by Segment

Here are some suggested pathways to develop based on which segment a respondent falls into.

1. Haters:

   a. Send an immediate email response stating, "Thank you for your honest feedback, [First Name]. It is greatly appreciated. While we strive to deliver exceptional experiences, we missed the mark and we're sorry that your experience was less than spectacular. We will be reaching out within the next [X] business days with the goal of resolving any issues you experienced."

   b. You'll absolutely want to ensure that a task is automatically set for either a person or department to contact this customer. I urge you to have a goal of contacting them within twenty-four hours. The faster you can contact this person, the better. Do not use automation from this point forward. It only creates more displeasure and agitation, making the customer feel less important. Human interaction is critical here, and empowering your people to make decisions quickly to remedy the situation is only to your advantage.

2. At-risk customers:

   a. Send an immediate email response including acknowledgment that the company missed the mark in delivering an exceptional experience, and then ensure them that they have been heard and someone will respond.

   b. Have someone reach out to them within the next business day.

3. Lovers:

   a. Thank them and restate how your company is doing its best to solve the Great Travesty and improving the lives of valued customers just like them.

   b. After a short delay (perhaps a few days), invite these customers to be a featured success story so your business can help reach more people like them and transform their lives. Your customer's story will inspire those still suffering from whatever pain point that customer had before your business.

   c. Whether they choose to act or not on the invitation to record a success story, you'll then ask them to refer their family, friends, and colleagues, and you'll give them a reward with real value in return. Offering a discount for them to buy more of your products or services tends to come off as disingenuous. So do your best to reward them after they have met your referral rules. Provide examples of great times and opportunities to refer people so they don't have to try and remember to refer your business or struggle with what to say about your business or its services or products.

CHAPTER 16

Stages 8 and 9: Recommitment and Winback

Not all love is lost when things don't work out with those
you love, as long as you've got a plan to win them back—
whether that be the next sale or the first sale.

STAGES 8 AND 9 OF THE Marketing RAMP work in tandem to target
selling to (a) customers who have already purchased from you and remain
active and (b) the prospects in the database who are inactive but remain
subscribed. Both stages are about taking advantage of existing leads rather
than letting them fall to the wayside in the pursuit of new prospects. I go
through both of these stages in this chapter and in Exercise 13. Let's start
by looking at recommitment.

STAGE 8: RECOMMITMENT

Stage 8 (see Figure 16.1) is called Recommitment because every time
a person considers giving more of their money to a company, they
are making a concerted recommitment to us, and we must earn their
allegiance every time. That's why the last portion of lovers and haters

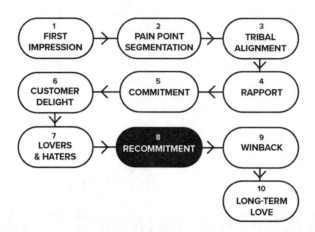

Figure 16.1. Stage 8 of the ten stages in the relationship journey: recommitment.

dovetails right into this stage. There are also strong undertones of customer delight here, but with a recommit twist.

In making this choice, the customer will reevaluate the exchange of value taking place, which leads them to one of the following decisions:

1. The relationship is fairly balanced, with an equal exchange of value for their money. Typically, this is where neutral or at-risk customers sit.

2. They paid more money than the value they received, creating an imbalance in favor of the company. This is where our haters reside.

3. The value they are getting far outweighs what they are paying, and the imbalance is in their favor. This is where our lovers live, and where we want most of our customers to be.

As we did back in Stage 6: Customer Delight, here in Stage 8, it's time to think about the activities and events that need to happen once a sale is made. This time, however, we should emphasize that the customer is at risk of losing what they gained from purchasing your original product or service. The reminder of what the pain was like before they experienced your solution and how it felt to have their pain removed should be powerfully communicated. Another avenue is increasing the ties between existing customers and your organization, which is captured by the ascension ladder principle, which I discuss next.

BUILDING AN ASCENSION PATH STRATEGY

Suppose you own a restaurant. You want each customer who comes in to order a drink and then an appetizer, an entree, another beverage, and a dessert. That progression from first beverage to dessert is an example of an *ascension path*: getting a customer to proceed along a pathway where they purchase additional products or services and increase their ties to your organization as well as generate higher profit margins for your business. There will likely be systems in place designed to enhance their dining experience, all while encouraging them along the ascension path. Using a product-based example, let's consider a smartphone. In addition to the device itself, customers can be encouraged to purchase insurance, charging accessories, wireless headphones, and a protective case.

The questions and examples in Table 16.1 will help you build an ascension path strategy so you can become more effective in Stage 8.

RECOMMITMENT IN ACTION

One of my clients is a *New York Times* best-selling author and Harvard professor who gives a master class in negotiation. His business trains individuals and executives on how to successfully negotiate when the stakes are high. He reached out to us after the massive success of his book with the hope that implementing a Marketing RAMP would deliver consistent selling opportunities after customers made the initial purchase.

We knew that his Stage 8: Recommitment had to be airtight. The RAMP needed to communicate that an ongoing coaching package—which could be done virtually and at scale—was necessary for customers

TABLE 16.1. ASCENSION LADDER STRATEGY COMPONENTS

Component	Examples
What is the most natural sequence of products or services and add-ons for your customers (the ascension path)?	A college student ascends from freshman to sophomore year; an iPhone model 19 user ascends to an iPhone model 20.
Is there a complementary product or service that could be sold either separately or in conjunction with this next sale?	After a haircut, offer hair products like shampoo or styling products; after buying an airline ticket, offer a rental car or hotel deal.
Based on the original product or service they purchased, what is the consumption timeline in which we should be making the next offer?	If a bottle of vitamins lasts thirty days and they did not repurchase at the end of that window, recommitment should launch immediately. If you purchased new kitchen cabinets, however, Stage 8 may be delayed for a suitable amount of time before making a complementary offer.
Is there any urgency or risk that needs to be conveyed if they fail to commit to purchasing our next offer?	When a thirty-day weight-loss program comes to an end, the customer must act now to maintain their progress. After purchasing a new phone, you can only get insurance coverage for the next thirty days, so act now.
Does the next offer add value to the original purchase they made so we can create a benefit story around the sale?	Offer a weekly cleaning service after a new backyard pool is put in; extend an invitation for an advanced photography course now that the customer has completed their beginner course.
Do you have success stories that can be used to promote the success of those who committed to purchasing the next offer?	A customer who immediately signed up for the weekly cleaning service when their new pool was installed and now enjoys summer afternoons in her backyard with her kids, confident her pool is clean and safe, and will be for years to come
Do you have any stories of those who did not take the next offer, experienced pain again, and had to come back to regain their current state (of happiness and removal of pain)?	Fitness customer who stopped his personal training sessions, gained weight, and lost stamina before he came back to start all over again

to continue honing the new skills gleaned at the in-person and online training events they initially purchased. But crucially, we had to remember that the audience we were addressing had literally just been highly trained in the art of negotiation. So, rather than relying on a technical or tactical approach, we needed to be speaking from a place of sincerity and make clear what was at risk of being lost.

The communications centered around the idea that, like a physical muscle, their new skills had to be exercised to remain strong. We outlined what they should be doing in the months after completing the course to retain their new proficiencies, knowing that the majority would have done little to none of this on their own. We highlighted how, given the nature of the material, allowing these newly invested muscles to atrophy would result in dire consequences when the stakes were at their highest.

It was wildly effective. The offer made good sense, and the customers saw that. The organization had already been charting success, experiencing massive scale at an incredible pace. But with a strong Stage 8 in place, it went from having no defined process in place for upselling to having a powerfully effective sales stage that was smart enough to automatically launch, start engaging, and sell without human intervention.

DURATION OF STAGE 8

There is no set timeline for the recommitment stage. It depends on your business type and what's being offered, among a slew of other considerations. The important thing is remaining mindful of what behaviors indicate a customer is open to doing business again. Perhaps they are reviewing pricing pages on your website or consuming content from your organization that is typically reserved for prospects making purchasing decisions. There's plenty of technology available to help monitor how people interact with your material. Once the trigger has been set off and the recommitment stage is officially underway, communications with that customer can and should be ramped up.

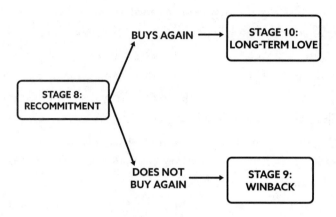

Figure 16.2. Stage 8: the process flow in your CRM.

Fortunately, the RAMP monitors this for you. It has been designed to automatically move your ideal customers from stage to stage, adding value and delivering a delightful experience throughout, while offering suggestions of what should be done at every critical touch point within the buyer's personal journey.

If the customer completes Stage 8 by making another purchase, they should be automatically moved into Stage 10: Long-Term Love. If not, then move them to Stage 9: Winback. The CRM flow is shown in Figure 16.2.

STAGE 9: WINBACK

As the name of Stage 9 might suggest (see Figure 16.3), the goal is to win back customers who used to buy from you but do not any longer and to target the people in your database who have remained subscribed to your communications but have never purchased from you. If you are a service-based company that provides proposals or estimates, this means you'll want to reach out to people who never responded to your proposal or opted not to go with your business. If you're an ecommerce-based business, you'll be contacting near-customers who abandoned their cart.

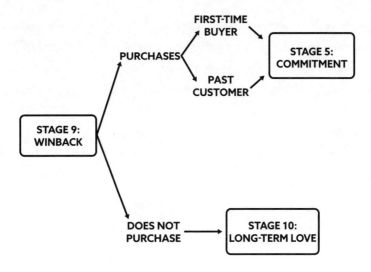

Figure 16.3. Stage 9 of the ten stages in the relationship journey: winback.

You already know that people who have arrived at Stage 9 have been moving through the Marketing RAMP and have been exposed to weeks of communications that include the Great Travesty, values alignment, pain points, aspirational outcomes, and success stories. Some have even experienced uncomfortable conversations where they've been called out.

Remember that so far, your Marketing RAMP has been attempting to move these contacts from being a prospect to becoming a customer. But they have not taken that step. You've also given them a chance to remove themselves from receiving your communications, but they failed to execute that action as well. That is a sign indicating they are still getting value from us and are interested in what we have to offer.

As you craft your first communication to customers or prospects in Stage 9, it's a good idea to check if the information you've gathered thus far is accurate. Surely your CRM and RAMP have done their best to capture information about pain points and solutions offered, but no system or human is perfect. So, in this stage, you should ask the prospect to clearly identify what their interests are.

Some will answer, and in your subsequent communications, you can make them an offer based on their primary interest. Ideally, there'll be some scarcity in the offer, such as a time-based expiration to its offer. Many people will not answer, however. In that case, they will be moved to a selected default interest category.

In either case, the emails you send should call on many of the assets that you have built and utilized earlier in the journey, such as the following:

- Success stories that address internal objections and promise to absolve pain

- Value in the form of a tip, video, article, or free how-to resource

- An explicit reminder of your secret sauce

Remember that relationship bank mentioned earlier? Our goal is to consistently make valuable deposits in it throughout the winback stage, so that when we include our call to action in each of these communications, inviting the prospect back into the fold, it feels like a fair and reasonable ask.

IMPROVING COMMUNICATION POINTS

The power of providing value in Stage 9 was made clear in our work with a venture-funded educational technology platform that works with school districts across the world. They had reached out because they were struggling to scale their business. It wasn't efficient to rely solely on a sales force to do the hard work the way they had been, since school districts have a complex sales cycle with multiple layers of decision makers along the way.

By working through their Marketing RAMP, they standardized the talking points and tasks across the sales team, enabling them to move swiftly through multiple sales conversations with school districts and principals at scale. After analyzing the data coming in, they were able to identify a critical pattern. Prospective customers often got stuck somewhere in the purchasing process and, as a result, missed the company's standard deadline for closing. Many of the sales reps lost interest in following up. By drilling down into that dead zone—the abyss where so many customers were disappearing—the company realized that often the person the sales team was communicating with was sold on the platform, but they did not hold the power to sign a contract or issue payment. That direct contact had to relay the information up the chain of command, meaning the higher-ups had to be sold, too.

The company realized it didn't want to leave that important round of selling in the hands of the internal contact, so they developed new assets—videos, infographics, and success stories—specifically catered to that exact conversation that needed to happen higher up the customer's corporate ladder. These assets did all the work for the school representatives, making them look like rock stars to their higher-ups. Best of all? Effective use of these assets removed the roadblock to a sale.

The strategy designed within this stage empowered the sales team to engage and sell to more prospects in less time. This made the sales team more effective when they were having conversations with prospects and helped the company to increase sales conversations without adding additional staff. It not only enabled the company to have more scale for sales revenue but simultaneously saved them money.

I've found that the best strategy is to cast a wide net when it comes to a winback. If a prospect has shown any inclination of buying from you and has yet to opt out of your communications, it's wise to reengage with them. The winback stage of the Marketing RAMP reenergizes certain customers who have drifted away while also serving as a list purge system, removing people from the database who have remained inactive through the maximum number of attempts.

If the customer ends up making a purchase, pick up with your Stage 5: Commitment activities (and also Stage 6: Customer Delight). If they do not repurchase, move them into Stage 10: Long-Term Love. The CRM flow is shown in Figure 16.4.

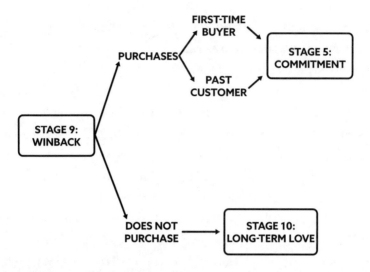

Figure 16.4. Stage 9: the process flow in your CRM.

 TOP TAKEAWAYS

1. You're doing your business a disservice if you assume that repeat customers are a given, even when it comes to those who classed themselves as lovers in Stage 7.

2. Customers who are happy buying from you should be placed into Stage 8: Recommitment. Here they will be sold to again.

3. Past customers and prospects who moved through the sales process but either chose another vendor or went silent on you should be placed into Stage 9: Winback. Here they will wait until your desired delay passes. And then you'll launch into delivering value, attacking internal objections, and urging the primary call to action.

4. Once your database has been automatically segmented by the Marketing RAMP in Stage 2: Pain Point Segmentation, then again based on those who purchase and those who have not, and

a third time in Stage 7: Lovers and Haters, you will have a robust series of customer and prospect classifications. You now have at your fingertips more sales opportunities and data—more than you probably realize—for what content or offers to create next within your current database. Use them all. This is your mined gold and all you need to do now is go collect it.

5. The Marketing RAMP deftly handles the distinct communication style and cadence necessary to make both Stages 8 and 9 of the customer journey run smoothly and effectively.

EXERCISE 13: STAGES 8 AND 9: RECOMMITMENT AND WINBACK

Here are the exercises you'll want to complete to develop your company's next stage of the Marketing RAMP. You can visit www.marketingramp. com and create your free account, where you can enter all your details within the Marketing RAMP software that's been designed to make creating your own RAMP incredibly easy.

Develop an Ascension Path Strategy for Stage 8

Answer the following questions to identify how to best expand a customer's ties with you:

- Is there an ascension path our customers are recommended to follow?

- Is there a complementary product or service that could be sold either separately or in conjunction with this next sale?

- Based on the original product or service that they purchased, what is the consumption timeline in which we should be making the next offer?

- Is there any urgency or risk that needs to be conveyed if they fail to commit to purchasing our next offer?

- Does the next offer add value to the original purchase they made so we can create a benefit story around the sale?

- Do we have success stories that can be used to promote the success of those who committed to purchasing the next offer?

- Do we have any stories of those who did not take the next offer, experienced pain again, and had to come back to regain their current state (of happiness and removal of pain)?

Develop a Winback Strategy for Stage 9

To help build your Stage 9, think through the following issues:

- For those who are entering this stage and have never purchased from you, would it be wise to run a smaller Stage 2: Pain Point Segmentation again to ensure that their pain point and your offers are indeed accurate?

- For those who have just come out of the proposal or sales process, how long should they wait and delay inside Stage 9 before this stage turns on and begins communicating again?

- How aggressive were your previous stage communications and offers? In other words, how depleted is your relationship bank account with these prospects? Your first few communications may be best served to deliver real value and delight before selling again.

- Is there a different product, service, tone, or method to sell to this population who have not been successfully aligned into your company's tribe and made a commitment to buy from you? Sometimes, completely rethinking how you are communicating is what's preventing you from the sale. This is the place to test your new copy, stories, and presentation of offers.

- For companies with sales teams, what is the best alternating rhythm for the Marketing RAMP to communicate with the prospects before the system creates a task for the assigned sales rep to then contact the prospect directly?

- What are other modes of communication you can employ at this stage that are right for your audience?
  - Direct mail
  - Text messaging
  - Phone calls
  - Recorded videos sent via email
  - Social media
  - Automatic addition to a specific ad set audience

CHAPTER 17

Stage 10: Long-Term Love

> You nurture plants, not people. You love
> people; and in return, they'll trust you, they'll
> commit to you, and they'll buy from you.

ON THE MORNING BEFORE MY WEDDING, I met my father for breakfast at a local diner in New York. It was the first time I'd seen him in nearly thirty years.

You see, my father had a lifelong career in the military, serving our country ranging from the Vietnam War to Desert Storm in Iraq. When he and my mother divorced shortly after my birth, he was largely out of the picture. As a teen, that was what I disliked about my father. He'd stop by with some random gift he thought was cool, with no idea if I'd like it or not (seeing as how he barely knew me). And then he'd disappear again, feeling good about himself for having fulfilled his fatherly duties. We'd both pretend we had a close father-son relationship for the half hour he was there, and then he'd leave again.

When I was fifteen, I told him I'd had enough, and that was the last time I saw or spoke to him until that morning at the diner. But because he's my family, I felt a strong pull to make things right with him, and thankfully, I was able to do so. We now have a wonderful father-son relationship.

There's a saying that anything in life that is valuable is not easily won. Meaningful relationships with anyone—your family members, your partner, your friends—require attention, care, and consistent effort. Without that, they begin to deteriorate. Friendships grow apart, families stop talking, and marriages end in divorce. Meaningful maintenance is not only crucial; it is critical.

This same principle from our personal lives must also be applied to our professional lives, specifically in the way we continue to engage with our customers and prospects. But the standard "long-term nurture" method of communicating with our contact database is broken. It's sporadic and random, focused much more on the sender receiving value than providing anything of worth to the receiver.

Something better is needed, and that's the goal of Stage 10: Long-Term Love (see Figure 17.1) in the relationship journey.

The content of this chapter and Exercise 14 has wide-reaching applicability, helping inform content creation, lead magnet development, social media strategy, email marketing topics, and even digital advertising. In short, long-term love is all about designing an *annual content production strategy* that delivers authentic value and fosters genuine connection with the people who engage with your business.

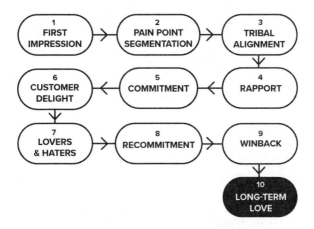

Figure 17.1. Stage 10 of the ten stages in the relationship journey: long-term love.

Having an annual strategy ensures that your contacts receive the optimal amount of repeated exposure, increasing conversions and sales revenue per customer. Let me explain why this is important.

CONNECTION MATTERS

Unlike the father-son bond with my dad, your customers don't have family ties to you and have no reason to keep coming back for more if your business is constantly getting it wrong. You need to give them a reason to stick around, and your current long-term nurture campaign certainly isn't doing that. Long-term nurture campaigns are just an ongoing onslaught of those dreaded old-school newsletters. Remember those things? Emails that would fire out providing no real value, only making withdrawals from the recipient's relationship bank account, and never making any deposits. "Sale! New product! Save 20 percent!" That's all these communications ever had and that's what just about every single long-term nurture campaign I've come across has done. It should be called what it really is, long-term sales emails. Besides, I always thought even the name "long-term nurture" was silly. You love people, you nurture plants. You need to ditch a poorly designed, outdated long-term nurture strategy and fully embrace long-term love.

This is not about selling anything. In fact, if you get this right, your products and services will sell themselves. It's time we shift to what we should have been doing a long time ago in the marketing world: acting with integrity, giving real value, and providing an exceptional overall experience.

DEVELOPING A LONG-TERM LOVE STRATEGY

Let's break down how you should approach developing a long-term love strategy.

Because the law of human reciprocity is ingrained in the Marketing RAMP, it's important to provide as much value as possible in each stage of the customer journey. In doing so, you're going to gain your customers' trust and ensure they want to continue doing business with you. The more valuable or generous the gift is perceived to be, the more inclined the customer is to do what you're asking of them because they feel indebted to you.

A cardinal rule of advertising is the necessity of repeated exposure. The accepted rule of thumb is that a prospective customer has to be exposed to your offerings at least three and as many as seven times before your messages resonate and the customer will take action.[29] Any messaging that is repeated less than three times to the same audience is lighting your money on fire—it's a complete waste of time. Sending the wrong message more than three times with no value while only asking for the recipient to give you something (time, action, money) is also equivalent to lighting your money on fire. The necessary continued communication to everyone in your database—prospects, past customers, active customers included—is at the heart of Stage 10: Long-Term Love. It's a stage firmly based around delivering real value and then connecting that value to the removal of the pain point, showing that reaching their aspirations is possible and then persuading them to take your primary call to action.

THE IMPERATIVE: CONTINUE TO PROVIDE VALUE

The human mind is an organizational wonder. It is constantly assessing data and determining what stays, what goes, what gets filed deep down, and what remains top of mind for fast and easy access. If experiences aren't attached to emotions and feelings, it's likely they will be dumped.

What this means in the marketing world is that when you stop providing your database value, then you've effectively ended the

---

29 Still relevant today, this rule evolved in the 1930s in the movie industry. See James Kaatz, "Marketing Rule of 7's," Illumination Marketing, accessed February 13, 2023, https://www.marketingillumination.com/single-post/marketing-rule-of-7s.

conversation and lost their attention. I don't care how great of a story you can tell someone; if you can't deliver them value and thus build trust, they'll never buy from you. Many times, I've seen great copy and wonderfully crafted stories in clients' marketing messages, but they don't convert into sales. They think they nailed their story, but those stories aren't selling. If you've experienced this, the problem likely isn't the story. It's likely that you never bothered to build a relationship with your people. The world is filled with incredible stories, and no one has time for them unless there's a definitive reason they should listen. It starts with whether you deliver value to them and if they trust you, and it ends with whether you'll transform them. Most of the world's most prolific storytellers were broke; don't let your business become the next starving artist.

Delivering value to a customer brings them positive feelings of gratitude and happiness, meaning they will more than likely remember you, they will be less likely to shop around, and (within reason) they won't be too concerned with what you charge them.

Unfortunately, many businesses get long-term love completely wrong. They throw content together with such little thought and care that most of the messages are junk that provides zero value. These businesses are simply trying to tick a box, assuming that they'll remain top of mind enough if something—no matter how pointless—goes out to their subscriber list.

Consider the standard business newsletters being circulated nowadays. Gone is the era when a newsletter actually contained news. Now, their content consists mostly of one thing, and that's a call to action. The entire correspondence essentially boils down to: "Buy this thing." It's a transparent sales tactic, backed by nothing of real value. This is exactly what we want to avoid.

Just as you're making a deposit or a withdrawal from your relationship bank account every time you make contact with a customer, every time you reach out to a prospect, you are giving them a reason to either love you more or love you less. There is no middle ground. Therefore, we must always be adding value relevant to their needs and their interest in the relationship they have with us.

It seems criminal how many marketers miss the mark with their long-term communications. It doesn't have to be this way. In fact, it shouldn't be this way.

DEVELOPING AN EDITORIAL OR CONTENT STRATEGY

A long-term love campaign typically includes a standard cadence and issues monthly, biweekly, or weekly communications from the company, depending on the type of enterprise.

There is a simple solution, and it starts with the editorial calendar. It's a brilliantly simple way to lay out content and a perfect fit for a long-term love campaign.

Editorial calendars can be used to map out future content ideas that match with the relevant times of the year. While creating an editorial calendar is a powerful baseline that many smart marketers already use, what I'm talking about here is a super-calendar that uses the knowledge you've gained about your ideal customers, pain points, and more to tie content to months, seasons, events, and our customers' hopes and desires.

If you know what your prospects will be thinking about seasonally, why wouldn't you talk about it? I've had marketers say to me that their customers are too smart for such a simple approach. But, as we already discussed, humans are tribal. People orient themselves around events, symbols, and ideas that are important to them. The human species craves rituals. Predictably repeating events, themes, and communications (when done right) are not only desired but also expected.

For just a moment, think about your morning routine. You do things in a specific order. It is, in fact, a ritual. This goes as far as the route you take driving to work, the times you eat, what you do before you sleep, when and how you exercise, relax, and socialize with friends—everything you do is a series of mini-rituals. Connecting your brand to those same important things builds trust and provides value to them in a way they're ready to receive.

Suppose we are the publishers of a lifestyle magazine. We know our ideal customers, and we know the content that performs the best each month is the recipes we put out. While creating an editorial calendar is a powerful baseline that many smart marketers already use, the RAMP has taken the proven format and improved it.

November is approaching and we're discussing what the main theme and recipe should be for that issue. If you're an American, your immediate thought is Thanksgiving. I didn't have to train you on that. I didn't even have to prompt, "What's an important event in November?" Your brain just went there. It's programmed into us, and we expect the majority of the things in our lives to be centered around this holiday. If, in November, there is a nationwide seasonal focus that neatly pairs with our product offering and appeals to our ideal customers, why in the world would we not write about it?

We decided that the centerfold article is going to be titled "The Juiciest Thanksgiving Turkey," and we're going to say it's the recipe our celebrity editor in chief uses herself every Thanksgiving. We'll explain in the article why this is her favorite and how it was her great-grandmother's recipe originally. We'll detail how she fondly remembered the smell of the turkey filling the house and the memories of all the family together, the joy it sparked in her, and how she has been able to pass this tradition on to her family through the decades. Building out a storyline around the recipe creates an emotional connection, which gives the asset being offered far greater impact and value.

At this point, if we simply wrote the article or blog and left it there, without inviting the prospect to opt in for anything, we can't get them into the Marketing RAMP, and the whole circular strategy breaks. And so we decide that the free asset is going to be the actual recipe. "Opt in, and we'll send you a PDF of the juiciest Thanksgiving turkey recipe in digital and printable forms." That way, when you're in the kitchen on Thanksgiving Day, you can have the recipe printed, or you can have it on your iPad. Either way, you don't have to worry about remembering the web page. We'll design it to look nice and encourage you to share it with your family and friends.

It doesn't stop there. When we deliver the recipe PDF, we include an email that says, "Having the recipe is one thing, but watching how our famous editor preps and cooks Thanksgiving dinner is going to make a world of difference to the final product. From November 1 to November 20, for only $99, you can access our step-by-step video showing you how to make the perfect Thanksgiving dinner that will bring more joy, smiling faces, and fond memories to your dinner table."

By this point, the article has explained why this is the best Thanksgiving recipe, we have given you the recipe in exchange for you opting in to the Marketing RAMP, and we're now extending a supporting offer with the product focus being that we're going to sell you an additional online course. And it all started with a simple email: "Hey, November is coming up. It's time for you to make an incredible turkey that's going to win over all your guests. Click here to read why this truly is the best Thanksgiving turkey."

I am a huge fan of multipurposing content. It's wise to use one piece of well-crafted content across a variety of channels. Why wouldn't you? You already have the content. You already have the lead magnet in place. By this point, you have your entire Marketing RAMP established to ensure that any new leads you reach are given an excellent customer journey.

Take the Thanksgiving article and make it an ad. Run it on all social channels and distribute it to your entire database. Now, not only are you delivering value to your existing prospects, customers, and former customers, but you're also mining for new leads by delivering relevant and meaningful value. Let's break this down into its simplest parts, so you can better see how to mimic the planning process:

- Month: November

- Season or event relevant to the audience: Thanksgiving

- Content: Recipe, built into a story explaining why it's special

- Lead magnet: Downloadable, branded recipe
- Offer supporting lead magnet: Online course covering the recipe and more
- Scarcity and urgency: Offer valid from November 1 to November 20
- Promotional outlets: Social, email, website, online ads
- Audiences: New leads who download the recipe from ads, the website, or social media who enter the RAMP at Stage 1; our existing audience already in Stage 10 who download the recipe and may opt into the online course offer
- Creation date and publish date: Thanksgiving content ready by October 1 to leave time for supporting assets, including graphics, ads, and email campaigns, to be ready in time for publishing to commence on November 1

You'll do this for every single month in advance. This way, you'll know exactly what content, assets, lead magnets, and even offers you'll be using for the entire year. Planning your content a year in advance using the long-term love formula, you'll be empowered to plan ahead, budgeting for time and cost. You'll also be able to run your marketing department like a billion-dollar brand that plans all its content, marketing, and offers many, many months in advance.

A RAMP FOR ALL STAGES

If a brand-new person who has never bought from us before comes into the fold through November's Thanksgiving content, the RAMP will know to put them exactly where they need to be. If they didn't take us up on our offer immediately after they opted in for the recipe, the RAMP will move them into Stage 2: Pain Point Segmentation to figure out what's most important to them and how we can help so we don't just assume this is what they want from us. If they do take us up on our offer and purchase that online course, they'll skip the RAMP's Stages 2 through 4 and be injected into Stage 5: Commitment, before then being dynamically moved into Stage 6: Customer Delight. Just as we would do if we were speaking to this prospect in real life, in a human-to-human conversation, the RAMP dynamically adjusts the conversation based on what the person is doing. In this way, the Marketing RAMP acts as a sort of brand concierge, guiding prospects and customers where they need to go in the most delightful way we can and at scale.

CUSTOMERS CRAVE CONSISTENCY AND CLARITY

By having an editorial calendar tethered to the events occurring in the real world, and by holding your business to a high standard by creating real value, you've ensured that the content you're putting out is perceived as relevant and is going to rank well with search engine optimization. Suddenly, you're much more accessible to all the potential prospects across the country who are going to look up a Thanksgiving recipe in the early weeks of November. You're covering all the bases, and you're nailing the long-term love formula.

Customers can sense when the communications coming their way are thoughtfully curated and logically distributed versus when they are haphazard or simply meant to check a box. We had a founder and CEO reach out to my agency who owned and operated four separate entities, with each brand meeting slightly different needs than the others, but with significant overlap. He reported that clients were getting confused about which was the best fit for them, and he worried the setup was creating gaps that lost him business. Worse yet, his marketing was in chaos. Certain clients were getting up to four emails a day (one from each entity) and being prompted to subscribe to a wide array of social media channels and pages that suffered from poor-quality content and irregular posting. His internal teams were burnt out and unmotivated to turn the ship around.

In its earlier stages, the Marketing RAMP helped unify the CEO's businesses under one name that would be recognizable to all types of customers, building out the brand's story and Great Travesty. But the true magic that was felt by the customers was in the long-term love. By following the model set out in this book, we were able to lay out an entire year's worth of content, offers, and promotions on a simple and logical timeline for the internal staff. The team was also equipped with simple metrics to understand what was working and what needed additional optimization. The result was a cohesive strategy that stood in stark opposition to what it was before, and one that simplified their internal processes, saving them tens of thousands of dollars in labor inefficiencies. The change resulted in higher conversions and reduced the communication fatigue that their customers were experiencing before we introduced the RAMP.

CONNECTING THE STAGES, CONTINUING THE CYCLE

Having an annual strategy ties into your foundational marketing. So many business owners overlook their editorial calendar and instead focus their energies on their social media strategy. As I see it, that's the wrong order, and it often results in a social strategy that is completely untethered and out of sync. Once you have put in the groundwork of building your Marketing RAMP and your long-term love strategy, what should go out on social media becomes clear. If you create one high-value, full-length asset, you can spin that copy into anything. You can turn it into a free mini-course. You can drip it out over social media over the course of the entire month. You can do whatever you want, and it all feels unified and cohesive because you have a central theme that you're working with.

Here in Stage 10 is where the beauty of the RAMP is thrown into sharp relief. By this point, you've worked hard to build your strong marketing foundation and get the framework for each stage of the customer journey in place. With the final component of the customer journey being the long-term love stage (where regular, relevant content creation takes place), there will suddenly seem to be a limitless number of ways to get new leads to opt in. Stage 10's editorial calendar framework produces a curated content topic, asset, and lead magnet. You'll already know for the entire year what content, lead magnet, and offer to produce.

Equally, each asset you put out then becomes its own brand-new Stage 1, and the process is perpetuated. New leads are being generated while the remainder of your foundation—Stages 2 through 9—remains intact. Your Stage 10 should be re-created with new content following the RAMP's editorial calendar framework once per year. Your Stage 1, on the other hand, will have a minimum of one new additional Stage 1 every single month. Over time, you'll have many, many Stage 1s, all feeding into the foundational Marketing RAMP's Stages 2 through 10. The CRM flow is shown in Figure 17.2.

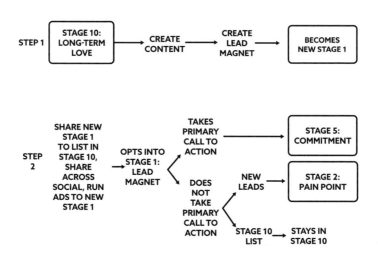

Figure 17.2. Stage 10: the process flow in your CRM.

This drastically cuts all the bloat and waste from marketing departments. You'll have your foundational operating system (the RAMP stages) for your marketing. Your team will be focused on producing the preplanned Stage 1 content, offers, and assets. And they'll be watching the RAMP stages for optimization based on how the system automatically segments and moves prospects and customers alike through the dynamic customer experience.

Once you have your entire Marketing RAMP laid out, including the customer journey, I suggest reviewing it once a year. Run through each stage and ask yourself smart questions such as the following:

- Are these still our ideal customers?

- Have their internal objections changed?

- Is our secret sauce as good as it can be?

- Is there anything going on culturally or globally that might affect their behaviors?

If you're committed to these regular check-ins, and you realize that the content you're producing is the gas that's powering your RAMP, you will not believe how far you're able to make it.

 TOP TAKEAWAYS

1. It's time to graduate from a smattering of empty newsletters to a strategic annual content calendar rich in value and effective in creating genuine engagement.

2. All people in your database should eventually come to live within Stage 10 of the Marketing RAMP. As your company grows and expands into new services and products, you can create another Marketing RAMP to meet the specific communication and experiential needs of those ideal customers.

3. The well-crafted copy from your editorial calendar content can and should be used across a variety of channels to get maximum mileage out of your hard work. Every month's content should be used across social, advertising, marketing, and digital communications.

4. Content should always have something of value (lead magnet) to give, thus requiring the prospective customer to opt in to consume it. This action (opting in) then launches the customized Stage 1 in which the recipient can commit to your primary call to action and thus be dynamically moved to Stage 5: Commitment. Or they will not take your primary call to action and will be dynamically removed to Stage 2: Pain Point Segmentation.

5. Your Stage 10 should be re-created with new content following the RAMP's editorial calendar framework once per year. Your Stage 1, on the other hand, will have, at minimum, one new additional Stage 1 every single month. Over time, you'll have many, many Stage 1s all feeding into the foundational Marketing RAMP's Stages 2 through 10.

EXERCISE 14: STAGE 10: LONG-TERM LOVE

To make the best use of your Stage 10 creation, we suggest you use a spreadsheet to organize all the details. Additionally, we've created the entire Stage 10 framework for you at www.marketingramp.com so you can simply fill out your details inside the free software.

You'll do the following exercises for each month. It is best to complete an entire twelve months.

-   Month: Name of the month

-   Seasonal focus: What holiday, event, or topics are top of mind for your audience during this month

- Product focus: What product or service should be complimented in your content

- Content topic: What is the story arc or topic of the content that you'll create is

- Free asset and CTA: A complimentary asset that brings additional value to the content

- Supporting offer: What you'll suggest they buy after consuming the content

- Supporting channels: Places where you'll distribute your content

PART IV

Running on the RAMP

THE EXAMPLES IN THE PREVIOUS CHAPTERS help illustrate the power of each of the components of a responsive, aligned master plan. But you may still be wondering how all the pillars work together in real life and how you can embark on this path in your organization. That is the purpose of the following chapters.

Chapter 18 presents two case studies that span the breadth of the RAMP, highlighting how the pieces work in concert to dramatically improve marketing results.

Chapter 19 describes the beginning steps you can take to launch your own RAMP and points out some of the resources available to you.

To end the book, I include a conclusion that describes how my experiences with RAMP implementations have led me to see that there is a revolution underway, not just in what customers expect from a vendor but in how businesses operate.

CHAPTER 18

Love in Action: Case Studies in RAMP Deployment

A WHILE AGO, A MORTGAGE COMPANY that specializes in providing active-duty military and veterans with affordable home loans came to my company with a unique challenge. It was successful, having grown year over year for more than a decade. When the founders decided to take a less active role, the leadership and management of the company were taken over by employees who knew the business and clients well and who had aspirations to grow and expand. The challenge they came to us with was three-fold:

- First, they needed to establish the brand to be able to stand on its own without the former founders, who held all the relationships and clout.

- Second, they had no differentiation within the marketplace other than specializing in loans for active-duty and retired military personnel, something that many other mortgage companies offer across the United States.

- Third, they had no actual marketing in place; until now, the company had relied on the former owner's relationships and referrals to generate business.

I'd be lying if I said this challenge didn't scare me a bit because of a perfect storm of complications. Yes, I knew the Marketing RAMP approach could improve an existing marketing department. But could it be effective in a company with essentially no existing marketing efforts? I also wondered about whether our Marketing RAMP approach could perform in such a specialized and highly regulated industry.

Ultimately, we clarified to the client that this was territory we hadn't ventured into before, but the new owners were eager to build their brand, create a marketing system that delivered qualified leads, and stand out among the competition that all looked and sounded the same. In this chapter, I tell the story of how the Marketing RAMP approach allowed us to reach those goals. Then, I provide a second case study that shows the power of aligning a business through a Marketing RAMP.

PILLARS 1 TO 3: CUSTOMERS TO LOVE, BRAND VOICE, AND PROPOSAL

Because the mortgage lender was essentially starting from scratch when it came to marketing efforts, the work we did in the first three pillars was even more important than usual. This business had never put much effort into identifying whom they wanted to serve and how to communicate with those customers, so there were lots of gaps to fill and very little to work with in the beginning. Here are some highlights of our work in these areas.

Pillar 1: Customers This Business Loved

As we and the mortgage company dove into the first pillar of the RAMP, *the people we love*, they identified their ideal customers as active-duty men and women who were first-time home buyers.

REMEMBER: FOCUS, NOT EXCLUSION

Though the mortgage company had a history of working with veterans as well as active-duty personnel, for the purpose of growing their business, they decided to focus on current military members. Obviously, they wouldn't turn away a veteran who wanted to use their services, but their marketing efforts would be focused on connecting with those who were actively serving.

We then helped the client create an empathy map for these customers: what they were seeking, what they were saying, what the buyers were doing, and how they were feeling. See Figure 18.1.

What the buyer is seeking

What they want, what questions they are asking, how to start

A loan to help them buy a house.

Benefits for serving their country.

Confidence that they are making the right financial decision.

What the buyer is saying

Pain points and internal talk tracks for objections to the sale

The process seems expensive.

The process may take too long, and I'll miss out on a house.

What are all the costs I'll have to pay?

What the buyer is doing

Research, product comparison, how they are shopping

Exploring loan options.

Trying to understand costs and timing.

Trying to find a partner they can trust.

What the buyer is feeling

How this problem is making them feel

Feeling overwhelmed by the stresses (both the loan process and being deployed)

Figure 18.1. The mortgage company's empathy map.

While investigating these customers' pain points, something interesting surfaced quite quickly. Many of the first-time, active-duty buyers would be deployed, in the process of relocating, or at sea either before or during their home-buying process. According to research, moving is the third most stressful event in a person's life, behind only the death of a loved one and divorce.[30] So the mortgage company would need to work extra hard to educate prospective customers about the process and the company's services so the customer would feel more confident in what was happening and would trust the company to help them, even if they were deployed.

Pillar 2: Brand Voice

In the second pillar, *our love language*, we helped the mortgage lender establish their brand voice and further honed their messaging strategy. They knew whom they were talking to, so it was important for them to get clarity around the company's core purpose (see Figure 18.2), what their customers value, their internal dialogue, and what kind of content they were consuming before applying for a home loan through the purchase of a home.

The company also boiled down the process into three simple steps (as discussed in Chapter 4). See Figure 18.3. Note that there are only two CTAs here: apply for the loan or talk to the team. This is the same in all this company's communications.

Based on the empathy map as well as the information from Pillar 1, we developed a warm, friendly voice that was semiformal, serious, respectful, and a mixture of enthusiastic and matter-of-fact. You can see examples of the resulting communications in Figures 18.4, 18.5, and 18.6. Note that the ad shown in Figure 18.4 is designed to help the buyer

---

30 University Hospitals, "The Top 5 Most Stressful Life Events and How to Handle Them," *Science of Health*, July 2, 2015, https://www.uhhospitals.org/blog/articles/2015/07/the-top-5-most-stressful-life-events.

Our Purpose

⋯⋯⋯⋯⋯⋯⋯⋯⋯⋯⋯⋯⋯ ★ ⋯⋯⋯⋯⋯⋯⋯⋯⋯⋯⋯⋯

We believe YOU deserve to own a home within the country you've helped defend.

Let us take the burden off your back.

Let us give you the home you've dreamed of & the benefits you've earned.

Enjoy a pleasant & easy experience from a team who cares about those who have protected our country.

Our appreciation of service members is deeply rooted within our company. We are dedicated to providing you with unmatched benefits & customer support.

Figure 18.2. The mortgage lender's purpose.

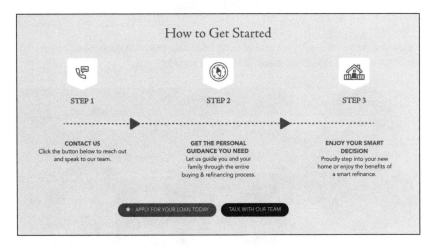

Figure 18.3. Three simple steps to success, as defined by the mortgage lender.

We believe YOU deserve to own a home within the country you've helped defend.

Since 2004, we've helped over two thousand veterans & active-duty members achieve their financial goals.

From landing your dream home to feeling confident in making the right refinance decisions - we'll make the entire process easy for you & your family.

★ APPLY FOR YOUR LOAN TODAY   TALK WITH OUR TEAM

Figure 18.4. Marketing copy for the mortgage lender.

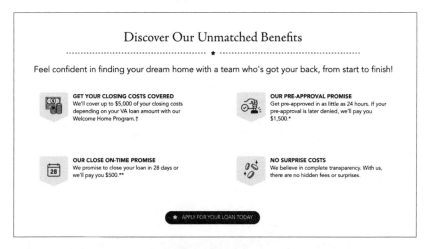

Figure 18.5. An example web page section designed to help overcome the prospect's hesitations (internal objections) about the mortgage process.

Figure 18.6. Image that addresses the prospect's feelings.

feel confident that the company is a partner they can trust, and it creates a connection by mentioning the prospect's service.

Pillar 3: The Proposal

In their work on the third pillar, *our proposal*, the mortgage company faced a challenge that many mortgage companies face: how to develop a secret sauce that makes them easily differentiated from and better than their competition when all mortgage companies are completely reliant on interest rates that fluctuate based on outlying factors.

Thankfully, the comparison between their competitors within the secret sauce exercise exposed their superpowers, the things that made them not only unique but also far better than their competition. The three factors of their secret sauce are the following:

1. *Innovation:* They handled the loans internally to ensure fast, accurate, and timely loan processing.

2. *Experience:* The uniformly positive experience their clients had with their staff and the education process throughout their journey.

3. *Success:* A high loan approval rate (and, thus, successful home purchase) for their clients.

Pillar 4: The Relationship Journey

As I discuss throughout the book, working through the first three pillars provides the inputs for developing the resources needed for the fourth pillar, the *relationship journey*. This is the engine of the RAMP. It's where everything comes together and the magic happens. Here are some of the highlights from this mortgage company's fourth pillar:

- *The Great Travesty* (the great wrong in the world that the company is working to overcome) was developed by looking at the

incredible sacrifice faced by every man and woman who is serving our great country. There is no guarantee that our country
will be at peace during an enlisted person's service, no guarantee
they won't be called into action in a foreign country, and ultimately, no guarantee this hero will ever return home should a
conflict arise. This sacrifice to ensure the rest of our country
remains free and safe at home should come with assurances that
when they want to enjoy owning a home, they can seamlessly,
simply, and at the lowest possible cost to them be able to enjoy
all the benefits our country awards to them. We summarized that
Great Travesty by stating, "You served proudly. Now it's time
you owned a home you can be proud of." The Great Travesty
aligned the mortgage lender's ideal customers by demonstrating
that not only could the company help them, but, most importantly, they understood them, respected them, and were going to
be their guide to see them through any and all perils of buying
that first home.

- *Stage 1: First Impression:* This company was competing in a
  sector where important factors were out of their control or the
  same for all competitors (such as interest rates or the prospective
  customer's credit history and income). The first impression was
  critical in making them stand apart, since all consumers seeking a
  home mortgage or refinance tend to be laser-focused on their rate.
  All else would be inconsequential if the company didn't differentiate itself from the moment of the first impression. Therefore,
  establishing a warm rapport and providing value instantly set
  the first impression that they were different, they cared, and they
  would work hard for the customer. In this case, we worked with
  them to showcase the free courses and content they had created
  to educate active-duty personnel about how to navigate and take
  advantage of all the government and independent incentives and
  discounts they had at their disposal. These incentives meant the

customers could purchase a home with the lowest possible cost, including having their closing costs covered. The company made sure that everyone who walked into their world had a great first impression, and it started with the gift of knowledge to navigate what seemed like an overwhelming process.

- *Stage 2: Pain Point Segmentation:* This company needed to understand what the customer wanted as well as what was preventing them from achieving that goal. Buying or refinancing a home is an incredibly complicated, drawn-out process that takes weeks, if not months. They had to quickly identify what the customer wanted and what had happened to them in their past to understand what internal talk track was going on in their heads and to show them that the company could help people just like them. The three pain points this company identified for their most-valued leads were (a) buying a home, (b) refinancing, and (c) learning about how VA loans and the home-buying process works. The content of the communications in this stage provided information as well as success stories relevant to those pain points. Doing this development work made it clear that the company's website had to be redesigned to be clearer and easier to navigate so visitors could quickly find the information they needed in those three segmentations.

- *Stage 4: Rapport:* The rapport stage is incredibly important when the time to purchase is long. Customers can get disheartened, become frustrated, and lose loyalty to the company they originally chose to patronize. So, during this stage, when the prospective home buyers were looking for homes, as well as going through the process to get approval of the loan, strengthening that rapport was critical for them. It continued to show that the business was there for them throughout the entire journey. That created a bond of trust and ensured once the transaction was done that they would leave rave reviews and refer their colleagues, friends, and family.

- *Stage 6: Customer Delight:* Each client was gifted a blanket for their home. In the corner, there was the company logo. Blankets provide warmth, comfort, and security, and that is what they wanted their new homeowners to feel in their homes as well as how they felt working with them.

- *Stage 10: Long-Term Love:* As months pass by after people have moved into their homes or refinanced their homes, the economy changes and their lives change. Some couples have children and realize they need a bigger home. Others have children who grow up and move away, and the time comes for the empty nesters to buy that dream home by the sea or simply move into a smaller home. Still other times, an addition, kitchen renovation, or advertised interest rates in the media promise lower monthly payments. Life goes on, and it's critical for the mortgage company to maintain that trust and bond. They would send tips about refinancing, when to refi, when not to, and what to look at when deciding to buy or hold on to the property. Additionally, they'd continually look at their previous customers' rates and personally notify them when they were confident they could get them a better rate. Talk about personalized service! Many times, those past customers were so delighted that there were no questions, no seeking other quotes, and they would immediately work with this company. It's proving real value, trust, and still delivering service well beyond the sale that separates the best companies from the ones that don't stand the test of time. It's experiences like these that create memories, and those memories will last and reignite the action the next time that customer needs to buy a home or refinance.

THE RESULTS

These changes in the mortgage company's processes, their communication, and their connection with customers led to astounding results. The use of free education classes for prospects who were considering buying a home using a VA loan drove the highest engagement in the company's history. Their new communication strategy, as well as their new website, immediately saw a double-digit increase in traffic leads and loan applications.

Within the first year of implementing the RAMP across their organization, they experienced a 180 percent increase in revenue, which was, by far, the single highest revenue in the nearly twenty-year history of the company. Everything worked so well in this first application that we then helped the mortgage company build out another RAMP for another type of ideal customers: realtors.

DRAGGED INTO THE TWENTY-FIRST CENTURY

The Marketing RAMP doesn't just improve marketing; it has the power to transform your business. Let me tell you a story that shows how I know this.

Built by Love worked with a hardscaping company that enlisted our services specifically because they recognized the importance of creating an incredible customer experience, and they knew they were falling short. The problems weren't obvious at first look. Their business was booming, their sales were steadily climbing, and they were confident they were providing a quality product.

But while the craftsmanship of the team was superb, there was chaos in the back office. Here are just a few of their operational issues:

- They were relying on manual spreadsheets for internal project tracking.

- They used traditional marketing funnels that ended after the project consultation had been scheduled (long before the customer actually made a commitment to purchase).

- They lacked the ability to track where projects were lagging.

- They had operational inefficiency, costing them time and money.

The gaps these problems created were losing them potential jobs and resulting in a choppy and off-putting customer journey. Even though business was good, they were aware it could be much better.

One goal of their comprehensive Marketing RAMP efforts, therefore, was to streamline the customer experience. It let each client know what to expect and when, guiding them down a path that felt comfortable and customized to them. This freed up project managers from fielding questions all day so they could instead focus on the work of staying on schedule and on budget.

The result was phenomenal. Within one year, the company went from charting $2.4 million in annual gross revenue to $4 million in annual gross revenue, with $1 million of the revenue being directly attributable to the Marketing RAMP.

Once the foundation was in place, there was room for yet further growth. Executing their RAMP created genuine delight in their prospects, and customers were deeply satisfied with their experiences. So much so that even in the middle of winter, when the ground was frozen solid and many of their services were suspended until the spring thaw, we helped the company design a RAMP for a sale for early bookings for pools and decks. The strategy was so successful that they made $100,000 in deposits for work that would not even start for another six months. In years past, the business had essentially ground to a stop in winter.

These changes have been so successful that they now have a year-long wait for projects to start. They decided to reduce the amount of their advertising spend because they were unable to meet the scale of the demand. What truly wonderful problems to have from a business perspective: "We must cut down our ad spend because we have too much business! We can't hire fast enough to fulfill all the orders coming in. We should lower ad spend until we have enough manpower to keep up with the pace of customers."

We all agreed that this was a much better problem to have than the one they came to us with. Yet a year after the Marketing RAMP was turned on in this client's business, those were precisely the conversations we were having, and those are the kinds of conversations and problems you want to have in your business.

IMPROVE YOUR OFFERINGS WITH OPERATIONAL SAVINGS

When you earn your customers' respect and loyalty and prove to them that you can be trusted, they're going to have an attachment to your brand, which means they will be much less price sensitive. People will be willing to spend more money to stick with a company they know and love. That is going to give your company the leeway and the margins to be able to sustain creating quality products. You're no longer going to be fighting a battle with the whole world. You can fully focus on making what you're putting out into the world the best it can be.

Look around you, and you'll see examples of this in many industries: Lululemon, Nike, Tesla, Apple, your favorite restaurant, and the service providers you entrust to provide care for your loved ones, whether it be a doctor, dentist, or nanny. *Build a relationship based on value exchange, trust, and an emotional bond, and you've got a customer for life.*

SIMPLICITY AND FLEXIBILITY

What I hope these two case studies—and all the other examples in the book—illustrate is that the Marketing RAMP framework is simple in philosophy and very flexible in its application. You can use it no matter whether your marketing efforts need to start from scratch or you need to improve existing efforts, no matter whether you're selling services or products. But how do you make it work for you? I talk about that in the next chapter.

TOP TAKEAWAYS

1. The Marketing RAMP approach can be used to fill gaps in existing marketing efforts or to build a marketing function from scratch.

2. The RAMP framework is so flexible that it can be applied to most businesses. However, the specifics of your plan need to be based on the specifics of your situation (your ideal customers, their pain points, etc.).

3. One of the most powerful benefits of the RAMP approach is coordinating efforts across the entire customer journey. By providing a consistent, customized experience for prospects, you can see greater engagement, improved odds of commitment, more-delighted customers, and more customers for life.

CHAPTER 19

Launching Your Own Marketing RAMP

When your people understand that the RAMP is their ally, not
their replacement, you'll break down barriers to ensure that
running on the RAMP creates success company-wide.

THE BOLD SIMPLICITY OF THE MARKETING RAMP approach is laid out
before you:

- Pillar 1: Figure out who your business loves.

- Pillar 2: Develop your love language to communicate with them.

- Pillar 3: Present the proposal of why they should come into your
  world.

- Pillar 4: Be a value-added companion to the customer on their
  journey from awareness to purchase to loyal customer. (See
  Figure 19.1.)

The natural reaction at this point is wondering if the Marketing
RAMP approach can work for you—or, better stated, what you can do to
make sure it does work for you. You may also be concerned about what

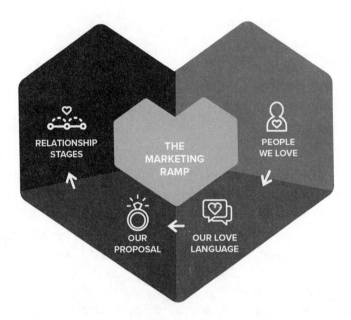

Figure 19.1. The value added by each pillar.

the process of incorporating the RAMP into your existing enterprise would look like. Can anything of your old approach be used? Should you assume that you're going to need to start from scratch? How do you communicate to your marketing team what the RAMP does? And, perhaps even more daunting, how do you communicate it to the other departments whose workflow it will affect?

In this chapter, I walk through some of the options you'll face in implementation. Because there are options. There is a way forward that will exactly complement where you and your business are right now and what it is that you need to step into a better, more intentional tomorrow. Just as the RAMP was built to do for customers, this book is crafted to meet you where you are—no matter where you are—offering tangible value. Here, I lay out some of the basic steps that my team and I use to identify what's working that should be applicable to just about any business. You can also use Exercise 15 as a model for kicking off important discussions within your company.

INVOLVE ALL STAKEHOLDERS IN THE EFFORT

Before getting into some specific tips for the steps you can take, let me start with one word of advice: use the development of a Marketing RAMP to unite all of the customer-facing operations in your company.

Think about it like this: The marketing department at a car company is not responsible for explaining to customers what the financing process is going to look like or when they're going to get the vehicle after purchase. That's not their problem. Their job is to create cool videos of the car in question doing badass things that make the viewer say, "Wow, I need to go out and get me one of those." As soon as the prospect is ready to convert, marketing hands them off to sales.

The sales department is responsible for closing the deal. They work out a financing plan and get the customer to sign on the dotted line. They don't care that there's a nationwide car shortage and the customer is going to have to wait months to get their new vehicle. They maybe didn't even mention it. It's about numbers. Quotas. Commissions.

Then the fulfillment or operations department steps in. They're unaware of what promises the marketing or sales teams have made. As far as they're concerned, their job is simply to get the car into the new owner's hands. That will happen when it happens, and if the customer must wait because there's an unavoidable delay, so be it. Each department is functioning as an island, in isolation from the others (see Figure 19.2). Gaps start to appear, causing prospects or customers to fall through the cracks and have bad experiences.

Having a Marketing RAMP helps combat the problems associated with an isolated or siloed structure. And it's why when my team and I are brought into a business to design and implement a RAMP, we encourage all stakeholders and their respective departments to participate. One of the ways the RAMP immediately adds value is by bringing a common language to a company.

In building their foundational marketing, that becomes the operating system. The marketing department suddenly needs to know what

Figure 19.2. The three core departments—sales, marketing, and operations—typically behave as isolated islands, preventing meaningful data from flowing to the executive team. The Marketing RAMP bridges this gap, creating alignment.

happens during the sales process. They clarify: "Okay, so you take a call, and then you create a proposal. What happens next? How long does that take for you to close?" The sales department might respond, "It could be thirty days, or it could be ninety days. It depends on the complexity of the sale." The marketing department would never interfere with the sales team's process or timeline, but now they know to be serving up case success stories and maintaining contact with the customer over what would otherwise be a dead period.

Next, the marketing team might reach out to operations. If they find out it's averaging seven days for the customer to receive their package after ordering, they can schedule a video to be sent out halfway through that time with instructions on how to use the product and imagery that's going to keep the customer excited during their wait.

Suddenly, the departments are working as a team rather than entirely doing their own thing.

Through discussions like this, the RAMP team helps build a common language and metrics. Everyone will know what the ideal duration for a stage is (how long you think it should last) and the max duration (the longest you'll allow it to last before moving a prospect into a different stage). This provides a uniform metric for the RAMP team to review outside of individual departmental metrics, and it gives them a shared language and process to do so. That forges powerful new connections across the business that didn't exist before, which will only further strengthen the brand and be palpable to the customers it encounters.

This also creates opportunities for better conversations with interested prospects. Armed with the knowledge of what's happening across departments, the marketing team can load the RAMP with content designed to inform the incoming customer of the process they're embarking on and preemptively answer questions they might otherwise bring to the sales team in the initial call. If the RAMP sends out an email with the pricing, the expected timeline, and everything else the prospect might want to know before committing to the company (and even throws in a few testimonial videos for good measure), the prospect is going to show up to their consultation much more ready to make a purchase than they'd otherwise be.

Any reservations the various departments might have had upon first hearing of the RAMP will surely melt away as they see the time and effort the system saves them.

The idea of carrying marketing outside the bounds of the marketing department in any way might sound alarming at first, and sometimes (but not often) it will trigger territorial feelings. But it's amazing what gets uncovered once everyone sees that the RAMP is not a threat. Instead, it's a way for everyone organization-wide to sync up and help contribute to a truly seamless customer experience, ultimately creating less work and more sales while making departmental quotas and goals easier to reach for all. Exercise 15 provides a framework you can use to hold these discussions with your team.

EVALUATING YOUR CURRENT ASSETS

Without knowing what's working and what's not, you're throwing spaghetti at the wall, and you're calling whatever sticks your new strategy. For obvious reasons, that is not what we want. When done right, marketing is an art form that is backed by a scientific approach to reviewing the output of data. It has nothing to do with luck. Don't let limp noodles determine your company's direction.

If you've been employing a traditional funnel approach to marketing, one of the primary things that will absolutely need to change is the way information is distributed. There is no world in which a barrage of templated, rigid emails can coexist with the dynamic nature of the RAMP. While the engine driving your marketing machine is going to change, we can rebuild the new engine from the same parts. Any videos, digital assets, emails, SMS messages, or copy that you like and can prove are working through analytics can be slotted into the Marketing RAMP in its rightful place.

The good news is that it's rare for a conversion to the Marketing RAMP approach to require a complete, 100 percent overhaul of existing marketing efforts. You will need to evaluate what is and isn't working in your current approach, look through the assets you've developed, determine how those assets are being distributed to the customers, and evaluate whether the type of language being used is appropriate for your ideal customer segments. After spending time with the material, we can isolate what should be carried forward and how it can be properly placed within the Marketing RAMP.

Strong content is often the easiest thing to carry over. That means ad, email, or call text that succinctly and accurately captures your Great Travesty or explains your secret sauce or is value-add collateral (such as articles) that helps educate your prospects.

Categorizing your existing content is a great place to start as you attempt to decide where the value lies. This effort will prove doubly helpful once you get around to identifying your ideal customer, one of the earliest steps in the RAMP. To determine what components of your current approach are working most effectively, put together a list of the major topics you address through all your channels of communication. Then evaluate how many people are coming in and what they're being drawn to. If there's a category of assets (or maybe even a single asset) that is a clear winner in terms of engagement, it'd be foolish not to carry it over into the RAMP.

Obviously, number of clicks or views is one metric of success. But look beyond those superficial numbers. Take the temperature of every level of customer engagement. Are the leads in your database opening your emails? If you're asking a prospect to do something like "Click Here" or "Book an Appointment," do they? If so, are they converting? Does it lead to a sale? Ultimately, that's what you need them to do. Metrics that reflect actions that indicate forward movement in a customer's buying process should inform your decision about what is working versus where your current system is breaking down and letting prospects escape before they become customers.

BUILDING YOUR OWN RAMP

I've been precisely where you are before, and I understand what you're feeling right now. A sense of accomplishment that you've just finished another book to help you obtain additional knowledge and skills to better yourself and your business. But also, a sense of overwhelm.

What do I do now? Do I even remember everything I learned over the time it took for me to finish this book? Where do I start?

Don't fret. Here's what I suggest you do next:

- If you haven't already done so, go to www.marketingramp.com and get your free account. This isn't a crude marketing ploy to get you to opt in. It is a custom software, costing six figures and requiring multiple years to develop, so you could have an online, guided process to easily develop your very own Marketing RAMP. We even built in options for you to add your team members to view and edit your RAMP. And you can add in collaborators with view-only access. The software was designed for collaboration specifically for the RAMP, so everyone across the organization can see the big picture and do their part to turn this operating system on in your business.

- If you have additional stakeholders in your company who need to sign off on projects like this, then start talking to them about the need to take a new approach.[31] That way, everyone in your leadership, sales, operations, and marketing departments is on the same page and understands how this will help each department, the company as a whole, and the customers thrive.

- Bring together a team from marketing, sales, and fulfillment and work through the exercises in this book.

A MARKETING RAMP BUILT TO LAST

Investing the time and effort to create a Marketing RAMP results in a foundational plan that you can continue to use even as you grow your business. It grows alongside you, both supporting and responding to the growth. This is a far cry from the marketing trends that quickly become outdated and must be replaced. If the Marketing RAMP is implemented once (and done right), it's something that you can run indefinitely. With the teams continually optimizing and enhancing it, it eventually gets embedded into your company's very DNA.

And it doesn't even have to be hard to accomplish this meaningful

---

31 Okay, here's the shameless plug: Share this book or buy extra copies and gift them to other decision makers who will need to be involved in creating and implementing a Marketing RAMP.

bond with your tribe. Once the Marketing RAMP has been built, sustaining the high quality your customers have come to rely on will be natural and comfortable. Your foundation will be set in stone, and it will come to be the only way you know how to do things. If you make sure that the communications going out your door are of value, if you're committed to the long-term love of your customers, and if you're creating new content regularly, people will keep on craving your secret sauce. They're not going to get tired of it.

 TOP TAKEAWAYS

1. Embracing a marketing overhaul doesn't mean you're necessarily starting from scratch.

2. Implementing the Marketing RAMP at your company will not mean stepping on any departmental toes but will instead foster unity and save time and effort company-wide.

3. Typical companies experience departmental isolation. Sales, marketing, and operations are their own islands with their own indicators of success and their own languages to explain those metrics.

4. The gaps between those departments are where the customers and prospects are lost. The Marketing RAMP builds a bridge between those three departments, and thus the islands all now connect back to the mainland, where the company can foster a streamlined experience for their customers and prospects as they move between the islands.

5. Effectively implementing the Marketing RAMP is not only a matter of deciding what to do with the bits of material at your disposal. It also fills in the existing gaps in the customer journey and, in larger organizations, unifies the departments to provide a previously unreachable level of service.

EXERCISE 15: INTERDEPARTMENTAL INVOLVEMENT

We cover the details of building the various components of the RAMP in the previous exercises. Sometime before or during the process of developing your own RAMP, you can foster interdepartmental coordination by getting your key players from sales, marketing, and fulfillment together to discuss questions such as the following:

- What is the ideal duration each step should take as a prospect moves through each critical stage in the buyer's journey?

- What is the maximum duration each step should take as a prospect moves through each critical stage in the buyer's journey?

- What assets and information are needed along each stage of the buyer's journey?

- How does the sales team close out the sale?

- How are new customers passed to fulfillment after the sale has been made?

- Are there opportunities to streamline the sales to fulfillment transition, with the primary goal of ensuring that your customer has a delightful experience?

- Are there any items, communications, or tasks your new customer must do before they can receive or consume what they purchased?

Based on what comes from this exercise and what is agreed on as the best holistic approach, build internal communications that are automatically sent to the respective people or department at each step in the handoff and the fulfillment process. Document any associated tasks in each stage in a master playbook that outlines the process for all involved.

Beyond Marketing: The Revolution at Hand

Love is the most powerful force in the world. Embrace it in your business, and it will thrive, standing the test of time and transforming the world.

ONE OF THE IRONIC DISCOVERIES MADE during the development of the RAMP approach was that the businesses that are most intentional about their marketing efforts are too often focused on the wrong things. While their marketing portrays quality experiences and products, the business is hyper-focused on profit margins and ends up providing subpar products and nightmare customer service experiences. Their mission and messaging are out of sync with their metrics—and the result is what many of us experience today with most brands we engage with as consumers.

Compounding the problem is increased automation as businesses actively invest in and create more and more mechanisms to *avoid* needing to interact with other humans. This is propelling even more frequent hellish experiences for consumers who continue to be pushed further and further away from actual meaningful experiences with the brands they buy from.

A revolution is at hand as younger generations demand more, and those businesses that focus on delivering quality experiences and products to people are the ones that will rise from the ashes of the current belief of profits over people and quickness trumps quality.

In this final chapter of the book, I explore this theme in more depth and make the case that all of us as business owners or executives need to be thinking about issues much broader than marketing.

RACING TO THE TOP, NOT THE BOTTOM

In its continual push to expedite processes and cut corners to make an extra buck, our society has lost a bit of its soul. Businesses large and small have forgotten that they are composed of a team of humans making products for other humans. This matters more than anybody seems to understand. People need to feel secure and looked after both in their personal lives and (perhaps surprisingly) by the brands they choose to give their money and their loyalty to.

This is undoubtedly a Great Travesty. But there is a solution to the broken system, one that is within easy reach. And all it calls for is businesses built by love.

Remember my ten-year, million-dollar quest to demystify marketing? It not only resulted in the formation of the Marketing RAMP but also cemented my opinion that the most effective brands, the ones that are going to leave the planet a better place as well as achieve robust business success, are the ones built by love. I believe in that idea strongly enough that it is what I named my firm. Love is the throughline that links and strengthens every stage of the RAMP, and it is a conviction that directs every decision I make while running my business.

I have met with many business owners over the years who tell me some version of the same thing: "My competitors keep dropping their prices, and I'm doing my best to match them, but I'm having a hard time staying afloat." They enlist the services of my firm, likely expecting—or at least hoping—that I do some marketing magic that increases their volume enough to keep them in the game.

Now that we've spent so much time together and worked our way through a whole RAMP and beyond, you must know that is not at all what I do.

Instead, I tell these business owners that their approach is fundamentally flawed. Once their focus becomes cutting costs, the quality of what they're providing customers is going to decrease. It's a race to the bottom. These businesses are forced to cut corners, and it always results in poor customer experiences and, therefore, a failure to build a tribe of happy, loyal customers. Instead, they churn through one-time buyers. This mentality is a cancer; once it takes root, it's incredibly challenging to eradicate.

The thing is, this scarcity approach could never work in the modern era, where products can be sent to customers from anywhere in the world in a single day, many of which are from countries where employers pay their workers cents per hour. They're going to be able to price-beat you every single time. The only way to win that battle, to win the whole war even, is to be willing to step back and think long-term.

To carve out success in a crowded global market, businesses must make the radical decision to treat their customers with integrity and respect and put love and care into the products or services they are offering. I am not naive. I understand that businesses need to make money and profit margins matter. However, I genuinely believe that once you commit to giving your customers quality products and invest in creating a smooth and delightful customer journey, you're going to stand out from the competition and find success you could only have dreamed of previously. In a world racing toward artificial intelligence with automation for everything and which removes the human element from nearly every experience, humans will want—they will crave—real connections with brands that deliver delight and prove that they care about their customers. Their customers are heard, respected, and loved back.

This goes against the current climate. We live in an era where intentional obsolescence has become commonplace. When my mother bought a refrigerator forty years ago, it lasted decades. Now my wife and I seem to be replacing our fridge every five years. That's not an accident. If we create cheap things, we make more profit per purchase, and we increase the volume of necessary purchases just to get by. It's a win-win, as far as capitalism is concerned, but a lose-lose for our customers and for our planet.

We need to break that cycle. We need to reevaluate our priority on profit above all else. We need to stop filling the world with trash. Companies racing to price-cut each other not only results in bad customer experiences but also exploits labor, pollutes the oceans, and dirties the air. Most recently, a shining example of a company that has embraced what the Marketing RAMP teaches is Patagonia, a company that places people and the planet first. It creates quality products, delivers great customer service, and most definitely is not the cheapest option in their product categories. Yet the company has continually thrived and has become a multibillion-dollar behemoth.

At the time of writing this, the founder, Yvon Chouinard, made the planet its only shareholder. In a world where fast fashion and cutting costs to produce products that won't last (and ultimately harm the environment) has been deemed a necessary measure to stay competitive, they stayed true to what I hope I and the Marketing RAMP have now taught you. And they are thriving while making the world a better place. I predict the company will experience incredible success going forward because they continue to understand a business built by love is the core for long-term success.

THE ROLE OF THE MARKETING RAMP

I believe that a Marketing RAMP can play an important role in forwarding society's movement toward a new, expanded commerce consciousness. No matter what stage your business is in, whether you're just starting up or making billions, we've created a path for you to be able to find success for your brand—and to feel good while doing it.

To that end, we have aimed to make this strategy as widely accessible as possible. We're offering a free version of the software that serves as a companion to this book. We're putting on online courses and workshops composed of professional marketers, copywriters, designers, and strategists who can help you build out your Marketing RAMP. Wherever you are in your journey, we want to partner with you and support the creation of your master marketing plan.

It can hardly be argued that business is the most efficient proponent of change. If we—if you—desire to change the world for the better, it begins with small and lasting shifts within our own companies. I am under no delusion that the marketing framework I have crafted will be the single answer, but it is my earnest hope that it will be one of the many catalysts for positive change that we so desperately need.

The best things in life are built by love. Commit to embracing this philosophy in every product you sell, every person you hire, and every communication you assemble, and watch as your business flourishes.

When your brand is focused on love, you gain more power than you could ever imagine. Your enterprise will be more prosperous, your employees happier and more fulfilled, your customers deeply satisfied and cared for, and the planet moved toward a path to healing.

When your brand is focused on love, when it is infused into every stage of your Marketing RAMP, you will never again fail at marketing. That's a promise. I urge you to now take action, step out into the world, and make it a better place with love firmly at the center of everything you do.

Glossary

Ascension ladder: This is a plan to sell and therefore ascend a customer from one purchase to the next purchase. An example of an ascension ladder is a college degree program giving you the required courses you must take to graduate from their program.

Asset: An asset is a valuable item or items used in design and marketing. Such things that are typically called assets may include PDFs, videos, logos, artwork, and photography.

Automated marketing: Automated marketing is typically managed and created within your CRM (customer relationship management) system. Automated marketing will automatically trigger an action when specific criteria are met. Such examples may include automatically sending an email after a prospect has opted in or a task assigned to an employee after a new sale has been made.

Brand: A brand is an identity within a company. When done well, brands build their own value and can demand higher prices. An example of a brand that lives under a corporation would be the iPhone. That is a brand owned by Apple.

Brand voice: Your brand voice is composed of the tonality, spectrum of formality, and personality that are communicated and perceived by the public.

Buyer's journey: The buyer's journey are the stages and experiences that a buyer moves through as they progress from being first introduced to your brand to purchasing and consuming your product or service.

Buyer's remorse: This is the feeling one gets when they regret their purchase decision.

Conversion: The conversion is the time a prospect has taken to convert into a buyer.

Conversion rate: The conversion rate is a mathematical formula to determine how many prospects are converted into leads. It can also be used for leads being converted into buyers. This number is typically shown as a percentage.

Creative: Creative is referred to as elements used within marketing copy, websites, and videos. Such items that would be referred to as creative would be web design (not the actual build or development), the story arc of a video, and how the email copy will be written, including stories that may be associated within the copy.

CRM (customer relationship management) system: CRMs hold the data of all current customers, past customers, prospects, leads, customer segments, and customer preferences. Usually, the more robust CRMs will include service tickets, analytics, purchasing history, and history of all communications.

CTA (call to action): The call to action is what you are calling your recipient to do either in your ad, your website, or your communications.

Customer delight: Customer delight is a strategy designed to delight customers beginning at their point of purchase and continuing through full consumption of the product or service. The intent of customer delight is to transform the customer into being a loyal, raving fan and to prevent buyer's remorse from creeping in after the purchase has been made.

Customer experience: Customer experience, also known as CX, is the experience your customer has once they have moved from prospect into customer. What they see, hear, and experience are all part of the CX.

Database: Your customer database is all your data that typically includes communications, transactional history, data segmentation, prospects, customers, and customer classifications. Customer databases are the core of CRMs and are usually integrated into other platforms, such as enterprise resource planning (ERP) systems, payment processing platforms, and sales team tracking software.

Digital marketing: This is marketing that uses a digital format, which may include SMS communications, website, social media, or email marketing and be used with devices such as computers, tablets, and phones.

Direct mail: This is marketing that sends communication such as letters, postcards, and sometimes promotional items direct to the consumer via postal service (also referred to as snail mail).

Domain: Domain is also known as the URL for most businesses. An example of a domain would be www.builtbylove.com, in which the words between the "www." and the ".com" are the actual domain. This is usually referred to as the domain name.

Ecommerce: The transaction or purchase of an item online requires ecommerce. This also can be used as the process of selling items online, as well as a term within the industry of businesses with the primary focus of selling their products online.

Empathy map: An empathy map is a visual tool that breaks the customer or prospect (in the case of the Marketing RAMP) sentiment and actions into four distinct quadrants. The Marketing RAMP's four quadrants are what the buyer is seeking, what the buyer is saying, what the buyer is doing, and what the buyer is feeling.

Human brain: The human brain is the informal name of the area of the brain formally called the neocortex. This area of the brain is where complex thought is processed, including (but not limited to) rational thinking, forecasting, judgment, planning, and making purchase decisions. This part of the brain within the Marketing RAMP is nicknamed the logical brain.

Ideal customer: An ideal customer is the person who is your ideal buyer. If you could have only this type of customer, your business would thrive and you would have loyal customers who love your product or service. They would happily refer you with little sensitivity to your prices. Ideal customers are also called avatars, ideal buyers, and many other names by marketers.

Ideal duration: Ideal duration is the ideal amount of time it should take to move a prospect or customer from one stage to the next stage within the Marketing RAMP. Your ideal duration is a hypothesis, something you strive for and that should be adjusted over time.

Integration: Integration in the marketing technology reference is the integration of two systems so that they may communicate with each other. Integrations typically pass customer data from one system to the next or will enable two systems that do not communicate with one another to do so.

Internal objections: Internal objections are what a prospective customer has in their head that usually speaks negatively about taking the next action. This internal dialogue usually presents reasons why they should not do the thing you are asking them to do.

Landing page: A landing page is a stand-alone web page designed for one specific action. It is designed to convert the viewer from their current state into the intended state. Typically, landing pages convert traffic that came from an ad into a now marketable state called a lead. Also, landing pages with sales objectives will be focused on moving the lead to a buyer.

Lead magnet: A lead magnet is something that the ideal customer finds value in and is willing to exchange their contact information for in return for the information. Typically, lead magnets come in the form of PDFs, videos, infographics, free courses, and types of quizzes or assessments.

List: List is referred to as your (usually segmented) list of people that you have classified as current buyers, prospects, and past buyers. You can have an unlimited number of lists, and most marketers have lists based on all sorts of classifications such as the amount spent, where the lead originated from, pain points, interests, and other things such as products purchased.

Lovers and haters: Lovers and haters are the people who have varying levels of satisfaction with your company as to how it pertains to them. Lovers are the highest-rated (most satisfied) customers, and haters are at the opposite end of the satisfaction spectrum (most dissatisfied).

Mammalian brain: The mammalian brain is the second of three evolutions of the human brain. It is formally known as the limbic system, and here is where the brain processes feelings and emotions. This part of the brain within the Marketing RAMP is nicknamed the feeling brain.

Maximum duration: Maximum duration is a strategy used within the Marketing RAMP to identify when a stage or a series of communications should come to an end. It is the maximum duration that you should allow to communicate that idea, request, or offer to the recipient before you transition into a state of agitation in the recipient's mind.

NPS (net promoter score): NPS is a calculation of your customers' level of satisfaction with your product or service. The Marketing RAMP argues that this is an outdated process and that the new approach should be followed in Stage 7's framework.

Opt in: The act of opting in is a prospect or lead that has provided their contact details and provided their permission for you to communicate with them about the content topic they've expressed interest in.

Opt out: The act of opting out is the exact opposite of opting in. Someone who has already been in your database and receiving communications from you has removed their permission for you to communicate with them.

Pain point: Pain points are the points of pain a prospect or customer has and wishes to have removed. The removal of pain is the leading cause for a prospect to convert into a paying customer.

Pipeline: A pipeline is a set of predetermined stages used typically in sales to identify where prospects and customers are as they move through a process. Pipelines are not limited only to sales and can be used for onboarding new customers, customer service or ticketing, courses or teaching or coaching consumption, and production stages.

PDF (portable document format): The PDF was created by Adobe and is a highly versatile document format used heavily in digital marketing when sending attachments that contain words and images. It ensures that whatever is saved as a PDF maintains its visual integrity when opened by the recipient regardless of their device or operating system.

Perceived value: Perceived value is value that is perceived by the intended recipient and is completely subject to their perceptions. What one person may perceive as being highly valuable may be worthless to another person who does not share the same views or values. Used within the Marketing RAMP, it is critical that you understand your ideal customers so that the gifts and offers you present are perceived with the utmost highest value. This offsets real costs. For example, if you perceive that having a red sports car is worth more than having a white sports car, you will happily pay more money for it even though it does not cost the automaker any more money to paint the car red versus white. (At the time of this writing, this is still a common upsell in all new luxury cars. The color red costs more, and the color white comes free of charge.)

Primary CTA: The primary call to action (CTA) is the highest-priority action you wish them to take and therefore will be the most visible and most repeated call to action throughout the mode of communication. Typically, CTAs are found in online ads, websites, landing pages, and emails but can be found in PDFs and all marketing and sales assets.

Prospect: A prospect is someone who has not purchased from you. They are a prospective customer. At this stage in the buyer's journey, they may be weighing options, learning more about what you do, or vetting you to see if your products or services can meet their needs.

RAMP: RAMP is an acronym for responsive, aligned master plan. It is the operating system that powers the Marketing RAMP and consists of four pillars. Within the four pillars, there are ten formulaic stages within the buyer's journey.

Recommitment: Recommitment is the repeated process of commitment. It can be repeated once (a second purchase), more than once (more than two purchases), or it can be repetitive and occur on a predictable cadence (a monthly subscription). The definition of recommitment within the Marketing RAMP states that every time a customer has made the choice to pay you again, they are recommitting to you, and this is a critical decision they've made and one that you must acknowledge and honor by continuing to deliver customer delight. It does not stop after the first purchase.

Redirect: Redirection is an action that typically happens after a form has been filled out and submitted or a purchase has been made. Although it can happen in other instances, for this definition it is redirecting the person from one digital place to another place. One of the places the Marketing RAMP suggests using a redirect is at Stage 2: Pain Point Segmentation. Once the prospect has selected their primary pain, they should then be redirected to a dedicated page and video that speaks to how your business can solve this pain for them. More about this is in the Stage 2 chapter of the book.

Reptilian brain: The reptilian brain is the oldest and first of the three evolutions of the human brain and is formally called the amygdala. This part of the brain primarily focuses on survival, detection of threats, fight or flight, sexual reproduction, and conservation of energy used for the brain's processing power. Regarding the Marketing RAMP, it is nick-named "the gatekeeper," and this is where the internal objections to try something new arise. Anything new is viewed as a potential for harm, whether that be perceived or real, and therefore it is met with objection in the brain's internal monologue.

Secondary CTA: The secondary call to action (CTA) is also known as a transitional CTA. This is a strategy used on websites when your web visitors are not ready to take the primary call to action. The secondary or transitional call to action will provide value for them without asking for such a large commitment. Consider the secondary CTA as asking someone out on a date, whereas the primary CTA asks the person to marry you. Much more risk and commitment are associated with the primary CTA versus the secondary CTA.

Secret sauce: Your secret sauce is the competitive advantage that makes you stand out from the rest of your competition. This also can be associated with a unique selling proposition (USP). However, the RAMP offers a more robust and useful way to implement the secret sauce versus the typically rigid and cold approach of a USP.

Segmentation: Segmentation is a method of classifying and categorizing information within a database based on any identifiers you wish to have. Segmentation is different from lists but usually used in conjunction when holding marketing conversations about whom to communicate with. Segmentation examples include (but are not limited to) prospects, customers, past customers, customers who bought X but not Y, and prospects who are part of a specific industry or vertical.

Sender reputation: Sender reputation is your virtual credit score for sending communications through text messages and emails. If you abuse your list of people with whom you are communicating by not removing them when they opt out or illegally obtaining their email addresses or phone numbers without their consent and then communicating with them, then you will damage your sender reputation. Once you have damaged your sender reputation, it follows you wherever you go. You'll have difficulty repairing the sender score, and you'll find it extremely difficult to reach anyone's inbox. Sender reputations are attached to domains, and there is no magic way to erase your sender reputation. So hiring a professional when doing mass communications or purchasing lists is critical to protect your business's sender reputation.

Spam: Spam is junk email, unwanted email that is usually filtered into spam or junk or promotions folders within your email's inbox. As a digital marketer, one of the worst things is for your business to find your communications ending up in the spam classification. Although this is not the only thing that prevents this from happening, the sender reputation is a critical component to ensuring you don't end up in the dreaded spam classification by the major email service providers.

Spectrum of formality: The spectrum of formality is a strategy used within the Marketing RAMP to measure the levels of formality in your brand's communication. Items listed in the spectrum of formality include casual to formal, humorous to serious, irreverent to respectful, and enthusiastic to matter-of-fact. This is a must-have for professional copywriters to nail your brand voice when writing communications.

Tribal alignment: Tribal alignment is the action of swaying the prospect to align their values with your tribe's values. Once you have been successful in doing this, you'll have die-hard fans and customers. Think of Apple users who are offended by the thought of using PCs, or the NFL's Dallas Cowboys fans at the thought of rooting for the Green Bay Packers.

Tribe: A tribe is what you want your customers and prospects to be aligned to with your business. More specifically, you want them to be aligned to your tribe because if they are aligned to your tribe, they will be more loyal. The fiercest of tribe members will be offended when your competitor's tribe tries to sway them. Classic examples of tribalism are loyal sports fans to their teams, Apple versus PC users, and Ford versus Chevy truck owners.

Web form: A web form is a digital form used with CRMs, on a website, and online. It functions so customers and prospects can input their contact info. Selections and comments can then be stored in a CRM, and actions can be triggered after the form was submitted.

Winback: Winback, in regard to the Marketing RAMP, is the action of winning back either a former customer, a prospect who has never purchased from you but moved through Stages 1 through 4 in the RAMP, or a prospect who moved through a proposal process and, for whatever reason, did not opt to do business with you. All these segments of customers enter Stage 9: Winback within the RAMP.

About the Author

DANIEL BUSSIUS is an award-winning marketing consultant. He is a serial entrepreneur and the founder and CEO of Built by Love, a full-service marketing agency. Since 1998, he has worked with more than one thousand clients globally, from Fortune 500 brands and celebrities to small business owners and start-ups. Daniel is the creator of the Marketing RAMP, a proprietary marketing process and software designed to provide a powerful operating system for any business's marketing department. He has been involved as a board member and advisor for $100 million software companies, publicly traded companies, entrepreneurial organizations, and *New York Times* best-selling authors.

Daniel is a cyclist, rock climber, hiker, and adventurer. He has competed on the television series *World's Toughest Race: Eco-Challenge Fiji*, which featured a four-hundred-mile race across ocean, jungle, and mountains. He is a loving husband and father, and he lives and operates his businesses in San Diego, California. You can learn more about Daniel at www.danielbussius.com and his agency at www.builtbylove.com.

DANIEL'S COMPANIES

BUILT BY LOVE AGENCY

Built by Love is a full-service, award-winning marketing agency serving clients across the world who want to build foundational marketing success, leveraging a team of professionals so they can best serve their customers, be market leaders in their industry, and enjoy predictable profitability.

www.builtbylove.com

DANIEL BUSSIUS CONSULTING

Daniel Bussius Consulting offers a personalized approach to marketing strategy services to a select group of clients who wish to work one-on-one with Daniel. Additionally, speaking opportunities and workshops are held under this division.

www.danielbussius.com

IN THE MIX PROMOTIONS

In the Mix Promotions is a boutique, experiential agency helping clients develop custom, unique incentive travel and brand activation events anywhere in the world.

www.itmpromos.com

MARKETING RAMP

The Marketing RAMP software provides the proprietary process featured in this book in an online format and is powered by artificial intelligence, which will create the marketing strategy and communications for business owners following the RAMP's trademarked framework.

www.marketingramp.com